EKATERINA LUKASHEVA

MODERN KUSUDAMA ORIGAMI

Copyright © 2015 by Ekaterina Pavlović (Lukasheva)

All rights reserved. No part of this publication may be reproduced, distributed, or transmitted in any form or by any means, including photocopying, recording, or other electronic or mechanical methods, without the prior written permission of the publisher, except in the case of brief quotations embodied in critical reviews and certain other noncommercial uses permitted by copyright law. The designs in the book are intended for personal use only, no commercial use without author's written permission. For permission requests, write to art@kusudama.me.

Publisher's Cataloging-in-Publication data
Lukasheva, Ekaterina.
A title of a book : Modular Kusudama Origami / Ekaterina Lukasheva
ISBN-13: 978-1516933686
ISBN-10: 1516933686

The origami models in this book were created by Ekaterina Pavlovic(Lukasheva) in following years:
2011: Apricot, Compass, Compass Star, Malachite, Phoenix, Phoenix Feather;
2012: Centaurea Cyanus, Centaurea Flower, Cream, Floweret, Ice, Jaciara, Rio;
2013: Bouquet, Celestina, Ice Cream, Jade Star, Lathyrus, Ornamentarium, Serenade, Snow Queen, Windflower.

Thanks to all the people who helped me making, test folding,
proofreading and illustrating this book. Namely

Elena Belogorodtseva
Ekaterina Kim
Boris Pavlović
Alena Rodakova
Natalia Romanenko
Tanya Turova
Jean Wallace
and all other people who inspired, encouraged and asked me to write a new book.

Photo credits

Ekaterina Kim: portrait on the cover.
Alena Rodakova: picture on page 52 (bottom).
Natalia Romanenko: picture on page 45.
Tanya Turova: pictures on page 30, page 34, page 36, page 57, page 61, page 63, page 68, page 70 and the cover.

CONTENTS

- **6** origami symbols
- **8** cutting rectangles
- **10** what is modular origami
- **10** about the author
- **11** modular assembly
- **12** octahedron (12A)
- **13** cube (12B)
- **14** icosahedron (30A)
- **15** dodecahedron (30B)
- **16** assembly hint
- **16** tips and tricks
- **17** book symbols
- **18** models

page 20

page 18

page 24

page 42

page 43

page 28

page 32

page 53

page 70
☆☆☆☆

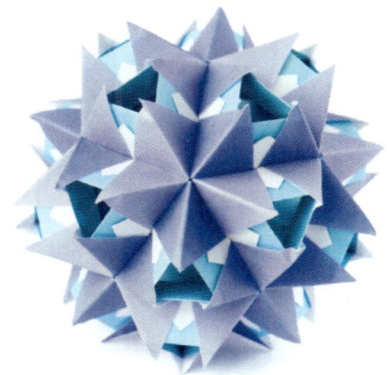
page 64
☆☆☆

page 66
☆☆☆

page 68
☆☆☆

page 38
☆☆☆

page 56
☆☆☆

page 45
☆☆☆

page 80
☆☆☆☆

page 78
☆☆☆☆

page 75
☆☆☆☆☆

page 76
☆☆☆☆☆

page 72
☆☆☆☆☆

Origami symbols

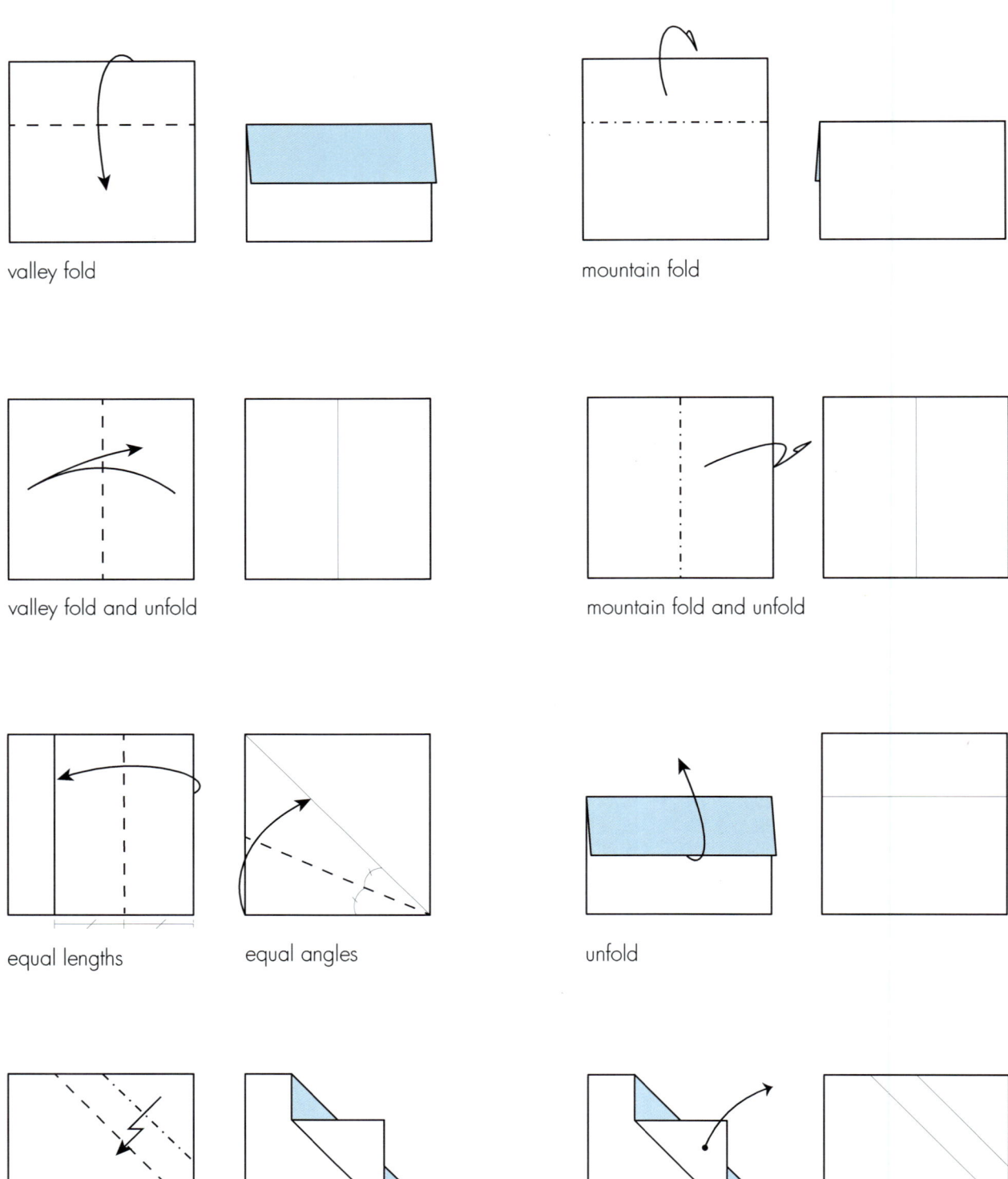

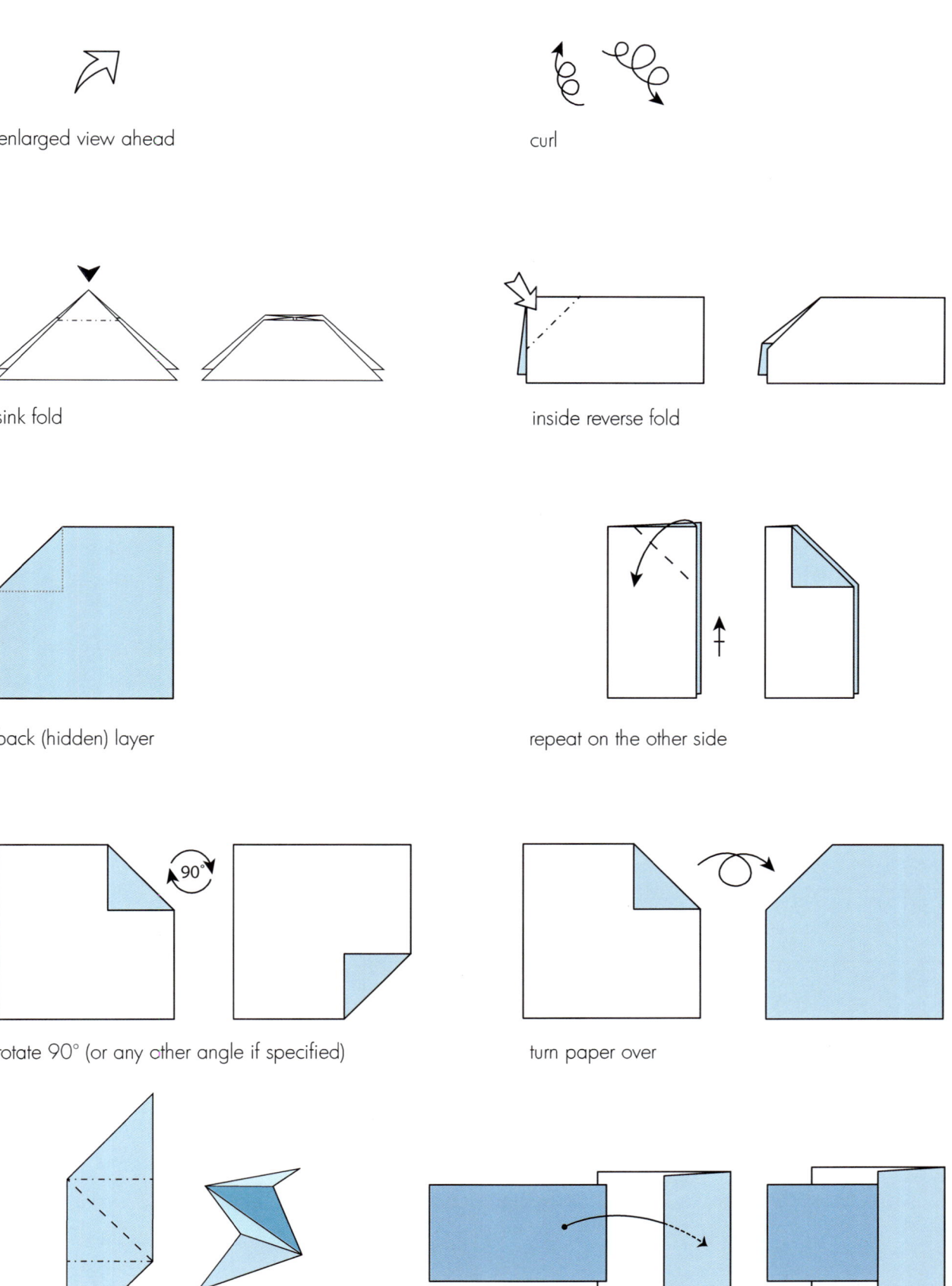

How to cut a...

1:2 rectangle (half square)

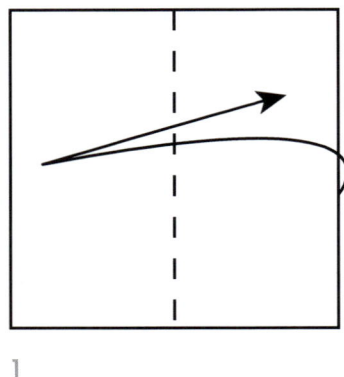
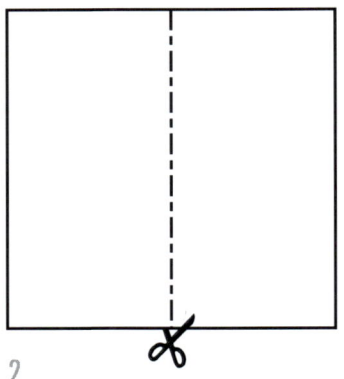

2:3 rectangle

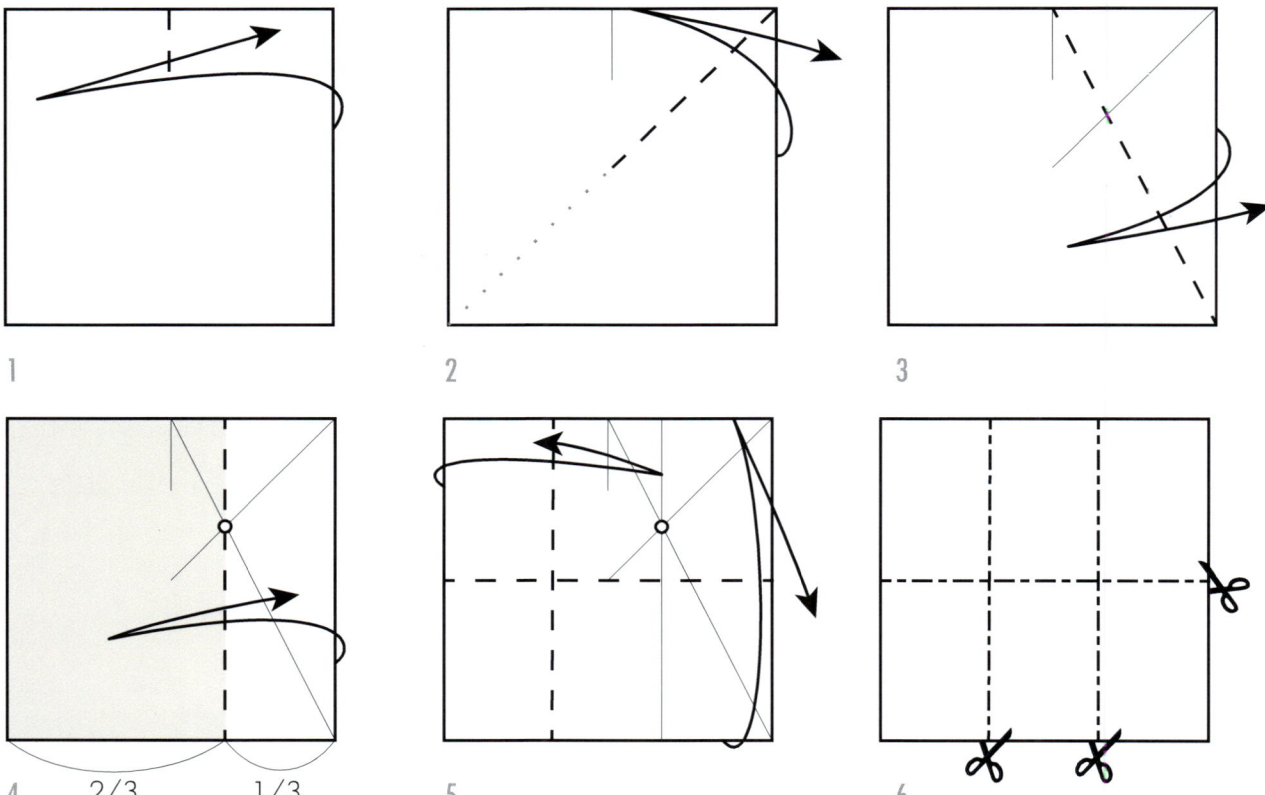

At step 4, the gray part is equal to 2/3 of the square's length, and the white part equal to 1/3. If you want a large 2:3 rectangle, cut the white part away at this step and use the the remaining gray area. If you wish to have smaller 2:3 rectangles, continue to steps 5-6.

2:√3 rectangle

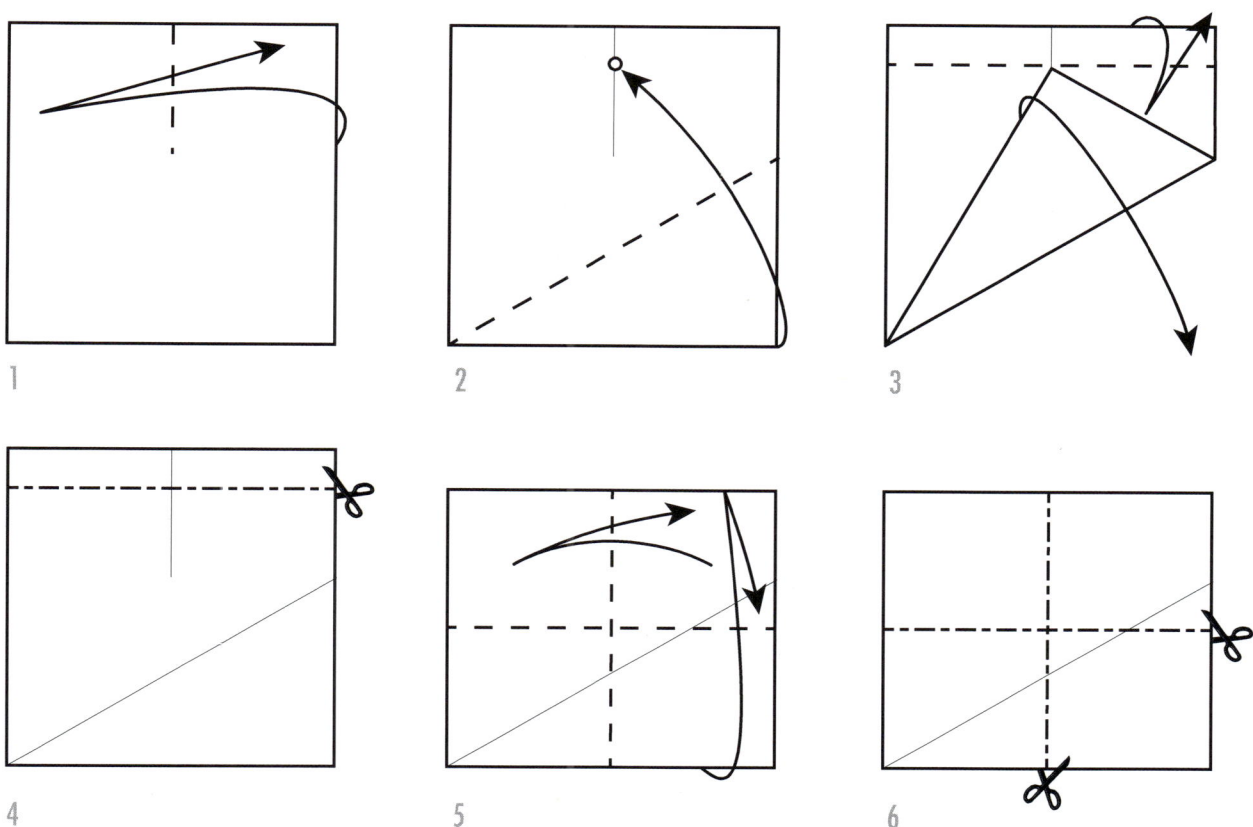

At 4th step you get the needed 2:√3 rectangle. If you wish to have smaller rectangles, continue to steps 5-6.

Modular origami

Origami is the art of paper folding. Traditional origami uses a single, uncut sheet of paper, whereas modular origami uses multiple sheets joined together to create a singular form. This method offers great flexibility in shapes you can achieve while keeping the single unit relatively simple. So if you dislike 100+ step origami diagrams still wanting the resulting piece to look intricate, modular origami is for you.

The figures created through modular origami are usually highly symmetric, because they are made from multiple equivalent units, or modules. The origami modules usually have special locks to allow unit-to-unit connection without using any adhesive. This feature of modular origami brings it closer to construction sets: you are just making the pieces of the construction set yourself prior to the assembly process.

There are several names for modular origami throughout the world. In the west it's referred to as modular origami, but in eastern Europe and South America, the Japanese word "kusudama" is is commonly used for ball-like modular origami figures. In Japan, the word "kusudama" originally meant "medicine ball", possibly referring to a ball made from flowers and used for incense.

About the author

My name is Ekaterina Lukasheva, but my friends call me Kate. I became acquainted with modular origami as a teenager; it quickly became my passion and has been ever since. As I grew up, I continually developed my modular origami skills, and at some point, I started creating my own designs. It is very interesting, since I compose the puzzles that I can then assemble into beautiful spheres. When I create a new origami model, I try to either make it look different from the existing models or make its modular locks different. In this book, I gathered models with locks that may seem unusual or challenging to you, but once you get the hang of them, you're sure to like them!

My first book Kusudama Origami was published in 2014 by Dover publishing. Besides that I usually publish my diagrams in various origami journals throughout the world. I have the website www.kusudama.me with numerous kusudama pictures, as well as a few free diagrams and videos.

I was born in 1986 in Moscow, Russia. Since early childhood I adored architecture and design art books and catalogs, as well as "entertaining math" books. I tried several hobbies throughout my life like construction sets, drawing, oil-painting, photography, modelling and... origami. The latter possesses me at the moment. For me it's the best culmination of mathematics, art and design. I gain inspiration from various 3-dimensional objects like flowers, cacti, architecture objects and stellated polyhedrons.

While I graduated as a specialist in applied math and programming and completed my PhD on differential equations, I don't feel any of these things are needed to make and enjoy beautiful origami. ;)

Modular assembly

The units presented in this book can be assembled in various ways. The assembly methods for modular origami spheres are based on the structure of Archimedean[1] and Platonic[2] solids. Each unit corresponds to an edge of the solid. The detailed assembly of these solids is outlined below.

There are two types of units in this book: 'edge' units and 'solid' units. The former act and look like real edges of the solids when you assemble the modules. But indeed the 'solid' units act in the same way: the only difference is that the final shape becomes solid, and the holes between the units turn to the pyramids.

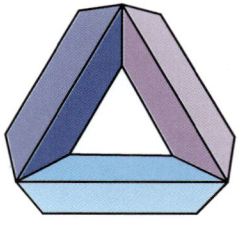
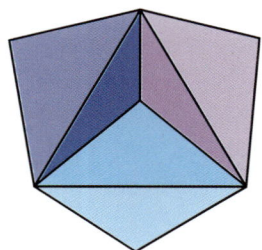

edge units   solid units

It means that the same assembly methods can be used for the both 'types' of the units. The following image illustrates the correspondence between units and the underlying solids.

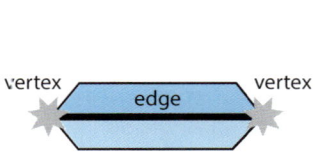
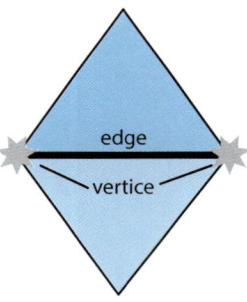

The methods below will illustrate the assembly methods for the edge units. But the same assembly schemas apply to the solid units as well. The assembly schemas are given symbolically, each arrow represents the unit's particular connection method.

---

1   Platonic solid is a regular convex polyhedron composed of identical regular polygons meeting in identical vertices.
2   Archimedean solid is a highly symmetric, semi-regular convex polyhedron composed of two or more types of regular polygons meeting in identical vertices. They are distinct from the Platonic solids, which are composed of only one type of polygon meeting in identical vertices.

Octahedron 12A method

A regular octahedron is an Archimedean solid composed of 8 equilateral triangles, 4 of which meet at each vertex. Since an octahedron is formed with 12 edges, you will need 12 units to complete a modular octahedron figure.

 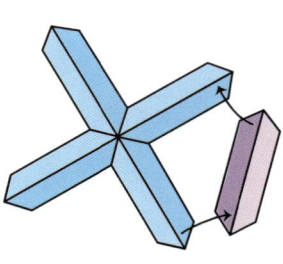 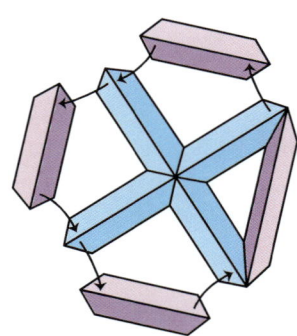

connect 4 units so that they meet at a single point

continue adding the units so that every 3 units form a triangular hole (triangular pyramid in case of solid units)

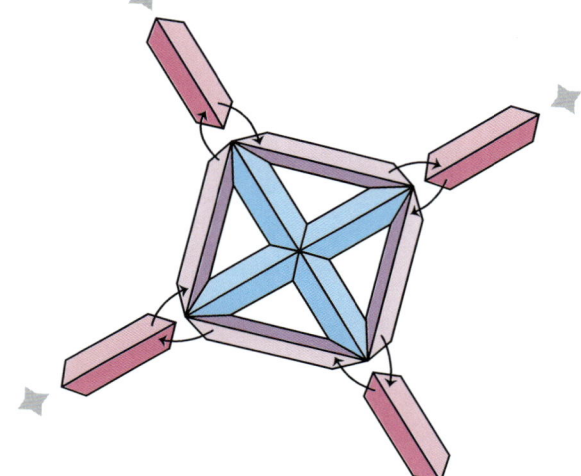

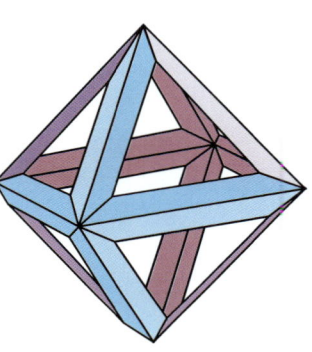

complete octahedron

add 4 more units so that 4 units meet at a single point each time

connect the sides marked with the stars in the illustration to one point behind, completing the octahedron

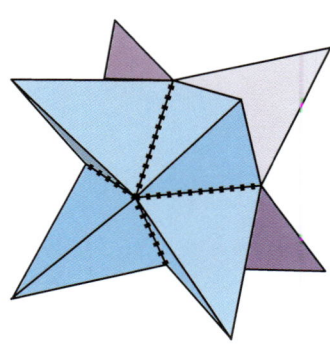

solid version of octahedron: dotted lines show the underlying octahedron

Cube 12B method

A regular cube is an Archimedean solid composed of 6 square faces, with 3 edges meeting at each vertex. Since a cube is formed with 12 edges, you will need 12 units to complete a modular cube figure.

connect 3 units so that they meet at a single point

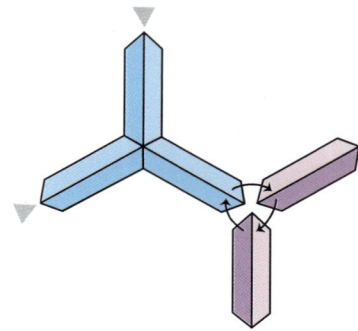

add units to the loose sides of the edges so that 3 units meet at a single point each time

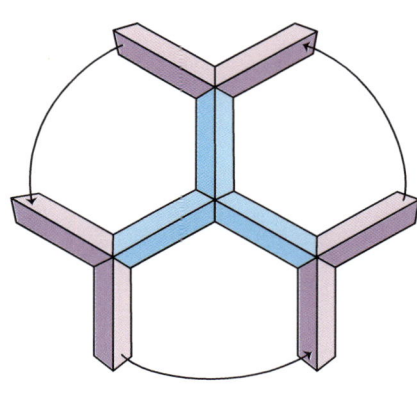

connect loose units as shown

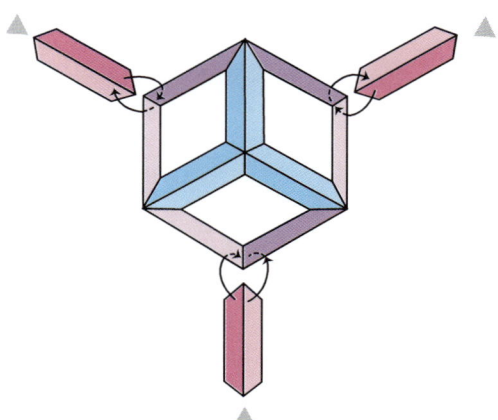

add the remaining units so that 3 units meet at a single vertex, connect the sides of the units marked with triangles to a single point behind

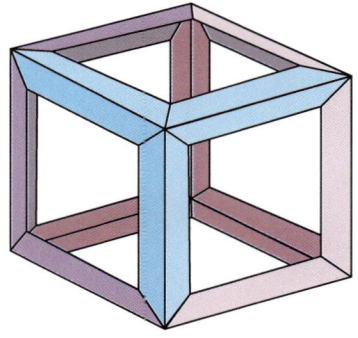

complete cube

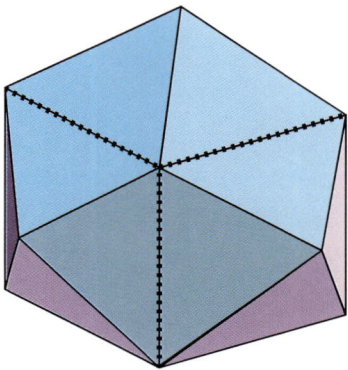

solid version of the complete cube: dotted line shows the underlying cube

13

Icosahedron 30A method

An icosahedron is a polyhedron composed of 20 triangular faces, with 5 of those meeting at each vertex. Since an icosahedron is formed with 30 edges, you will need 30 units to complete a modular icosahedron figure.

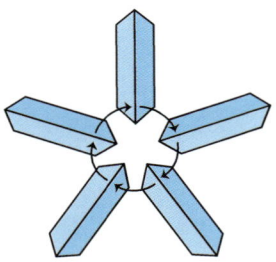
connect 5 units so that they meet at a single point

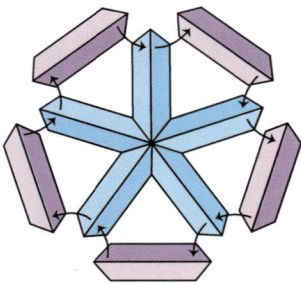
add 5 more units to form 5 triangles

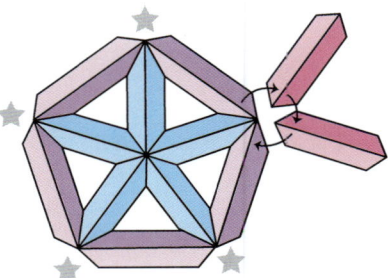
connect 2 additional units to every unfinished vertex, so that 5 units meet at a single vertex each time

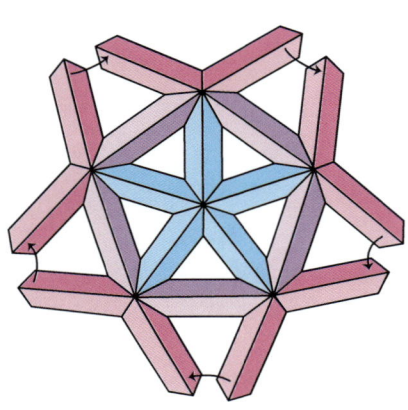
connect the loose sides of the units so that they form 5 triangles

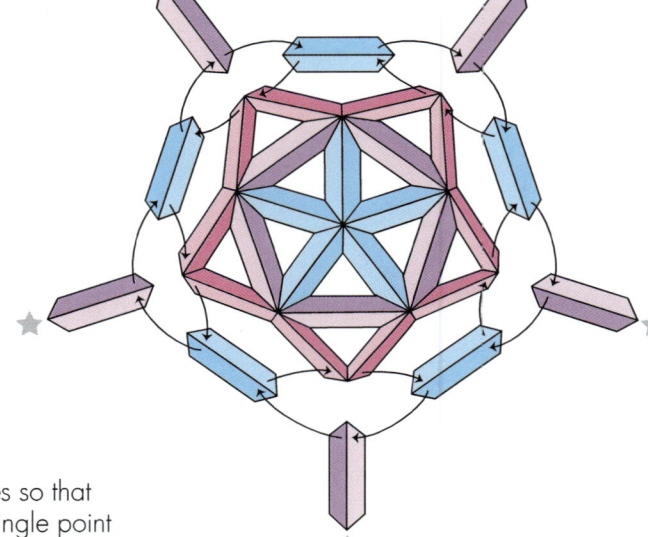
add units to the non-finished vertices so that 5 units meet at a single point the units marked with the stars in the picture should meet at a single point

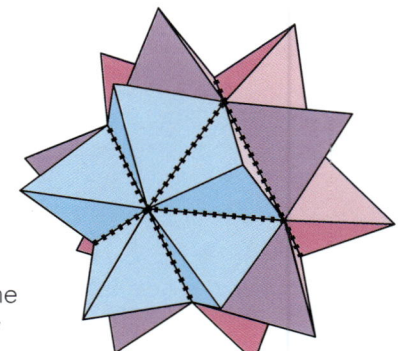

complete icosahedron (left) and the solid version of icosahedron (right)

the size of the holes as well as the sharpness of the spikes may vary from unit to unit

Dodecahedron 30B method

A dodecahedron is an Archimedean solid composed of 12 pentagonal faces, with 3 of those meeting at each vertex. Since a dodecahedron is formed with 30 edges, you will need 30 units to complete a modular dodecahedron figure. The assembly scheme described below may not be the most comfortable; while it illustrates the algorithm, the actual sequence of the assembly may be slightly different.

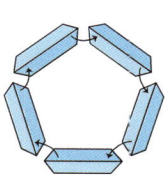

connect 5 units so that they form a ring

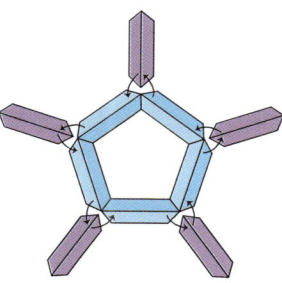

connect 5 more units so that every three units meet at a single vertex as shown

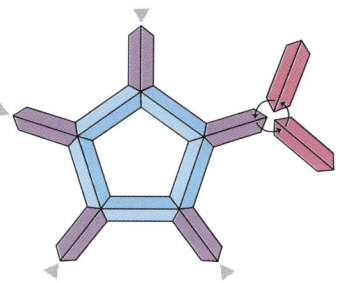

add 2 units to every loose side of the unit so that 3 units meet at every point

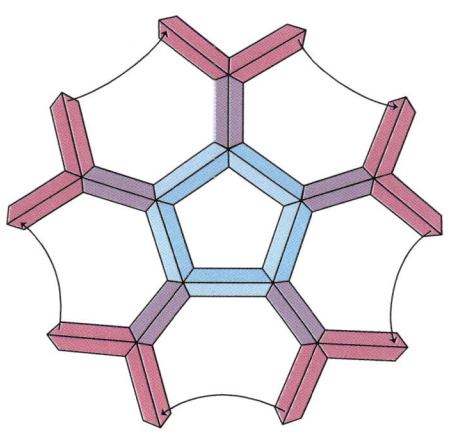

connect the loose edges so that you get 5 pentagonal rings around the central one

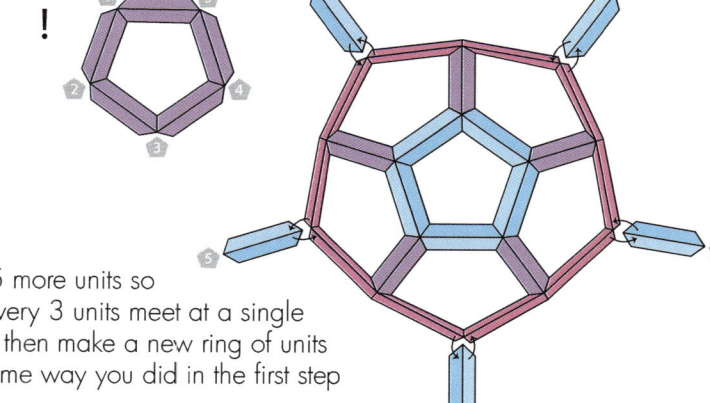

add 5 more units so that every 3 units meet at a single point, then make a new ring of units the same way you did in the first step

connect this new ring to the figure so that the numbers in the gray pentagons match up

this picture is to illustrate the structure only, as it is more comfortable to add the last 5 units one by one

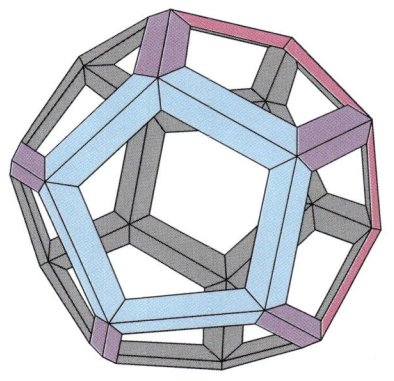

complete dodecahedron (left) and the solid version of dodecahedron (right)

the size of the holes as well as the sharpness of the spikes may vary from unit to unit

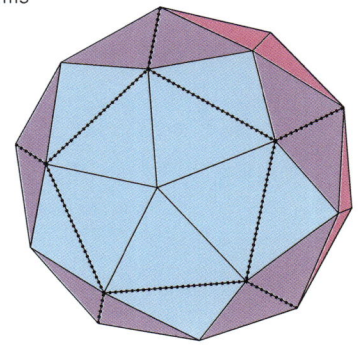

15

Assembly hint

Almost all of the models in this book (except Apricot, Compass, Malachite and Windflower stars) share a similar connection system which can look unstable at first glance. However, if you join the pieces as shown below, they will connect more stable, and assembly process will be more comfortable. The diagram below illustrates the modified assembly sequence for the icosahedron (30A method), but the same idea may be applied to any sphere you assemble. The concept behind this method is to try and finish the vertices of the polyhedron first. Thus, when you assemble an icosahedron, finish the vertices where five edges are connected. Since a "star" of five units is enclosed it becomes stable (steps 1-5 in the picture). Instead of closing the adjacent triangles, you should then assemble the next "star" (steps 6-10). Continue to assemble the model by finishing the vertices, proceeding in this fashion until the model is finished. As you go, keep in mind that the holes between the units should be triangular.

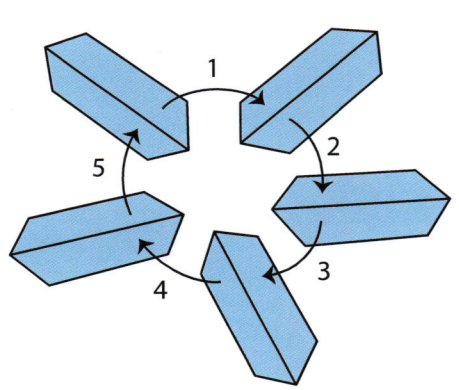
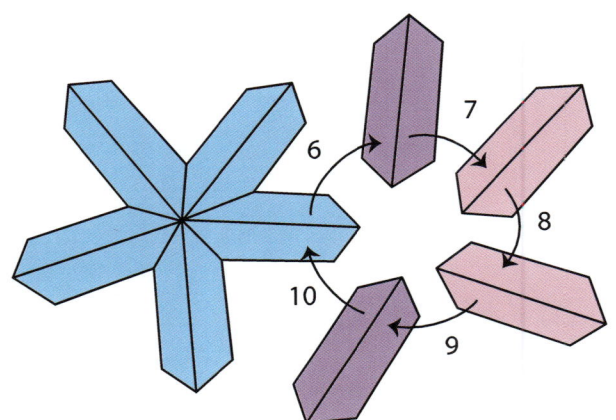

Tips and tricks

- Try to choose papers of the same type and weight for a single model. If you mix papers with different properties in a single model it may not only look inconsistent but may also lack symmetry.

- Try folding a test unit from lager piece of paper before starting the entire modular. It may give you a hint as to what paper size would be most comfortable for you, as well as how the color or pattern of the paper will appear when folded into a particular module.

- If you are not sure how to perform a particular step, refer to the next step in the diagram, as the illustration should give you a hint of the resulting shape.

- If you would like to use sticky notes for folding , you can apply some cornstarch directly on the adhesive, making it less sticky and more ideal for folding.

- Be as accurate as possible when making every single unit. The more precise you are, the better the final model will look. Some modular locks only function when your folding is very precise.

For precise and sharper creases use a folder or a wooden stick. You may find a special origami folder or use some clay modelling tools you can find in any art supply store.

A pincer or tweezers can be very handy during the assembly process or for curling the petals. Use it when you need to tuck the small flaps into pockets.

Paper and craft knives can be used for cutting paper.

A letter opener can be very useful for cutting paper when you travel; you can take it even on board!

PVA glue

Clips can be helpful to temporarily fasten the units for stability during the assembly.

The models in the book do not generally require glue for assembly, but if you are a novice to modular origami you may need some. If you want your kusudama have a better chance of staying together when handled by guests, children or gently batted by animals, add a bit or glue during assembly or to a complete model. Stick glue is better during assembly, while PVA glue (white liquid glue) can be used to fasten more permanently the complete model. Add a drop of PVA glue to the point where units meet to fasten the point. This glue becomes nearly invisible when dry, but be sure to test it on a scrap of your selected paper before adding to the kusudama.

Near the model name for each diagram in this book, you will find some symbols and other indicators with suggestions to help guide you in your paper selection, as well as the difficulty level and assembly possibilities for a particular model.

suggests the use of origami-specific gradient paper

suggests the use of paper with different colors on each side

difficulty level out of 5

recommended assembly method and number of units (see pages 12-15)

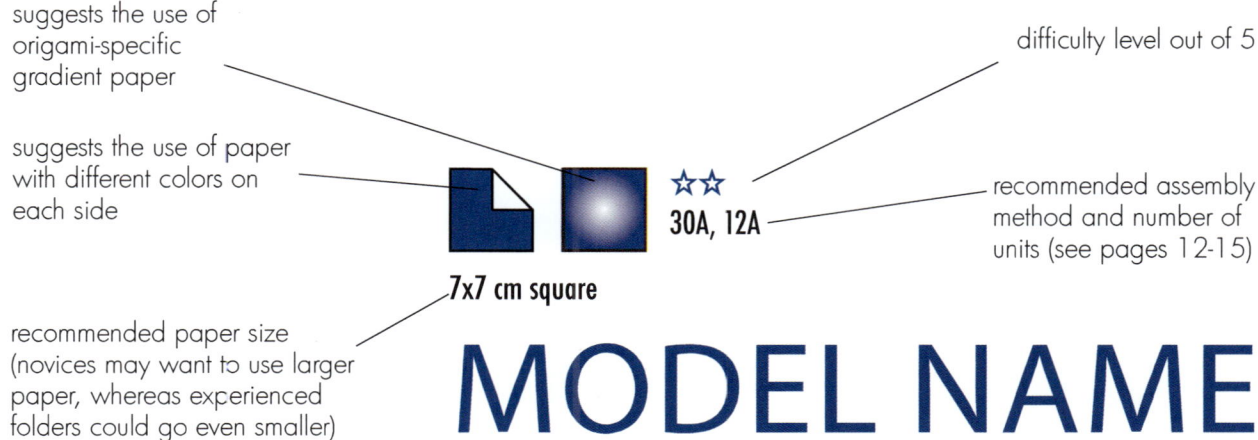

7x7 cm square

recommended paper size (novices may want to use larger paper, whereas experienced folders could go even smaller)

MODEL NAME

 ☆ 5-8 units

5x5 cm square

WINDFLOWER
STARS

This star is a perfect starter; it is easy to make and spectacular when finished. You may use these stars for many decorative purposes: glue them to the gift card or make a little brooch. You can make this star out of 5 or more units. I recommend making it from 5 to 10 units. The more units you add the fluffier your star will get. Use pincers to curl the loose flaps at the end of the assembly process.

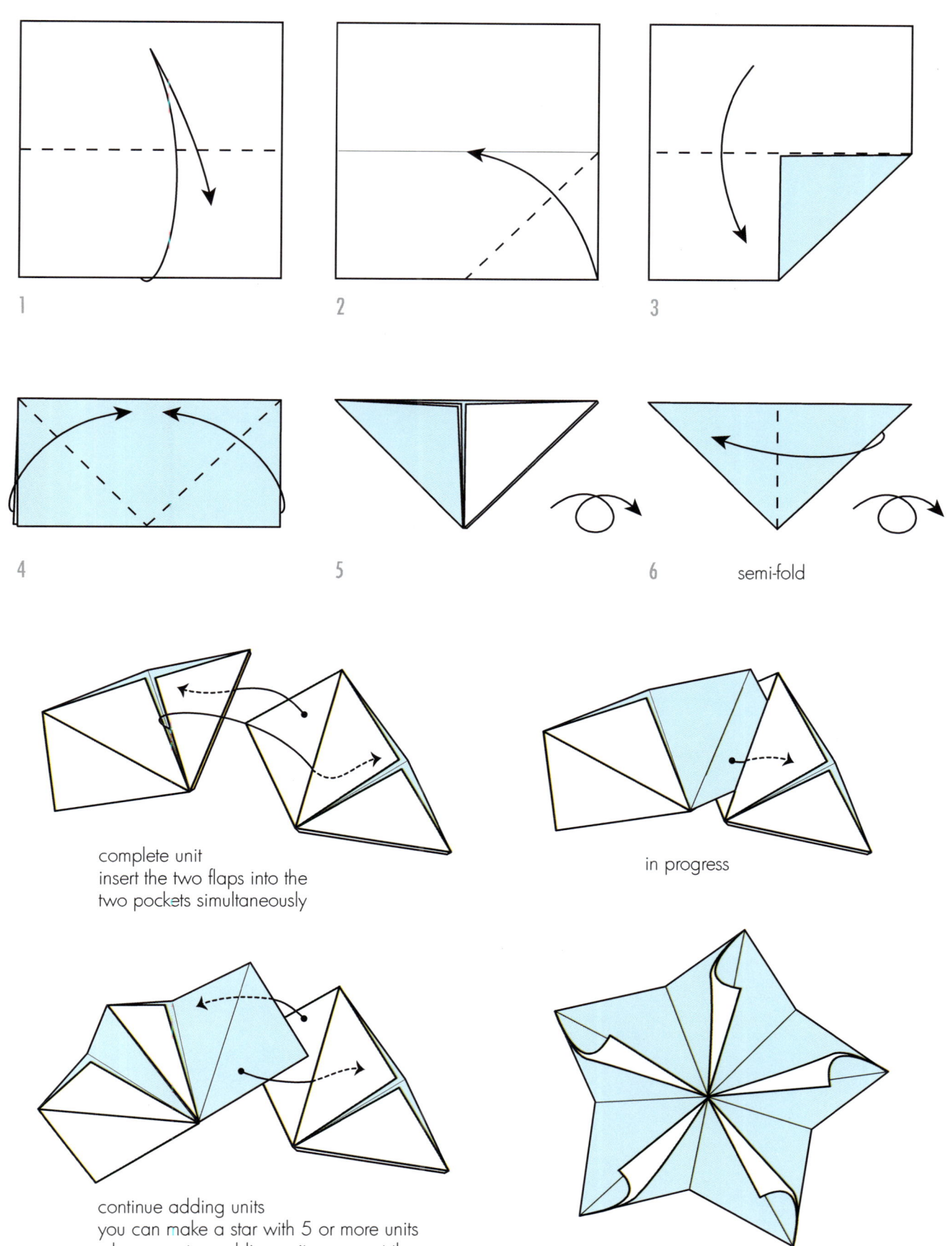

5x5 cm square 5-8 units

FLOWERET

1 2 3

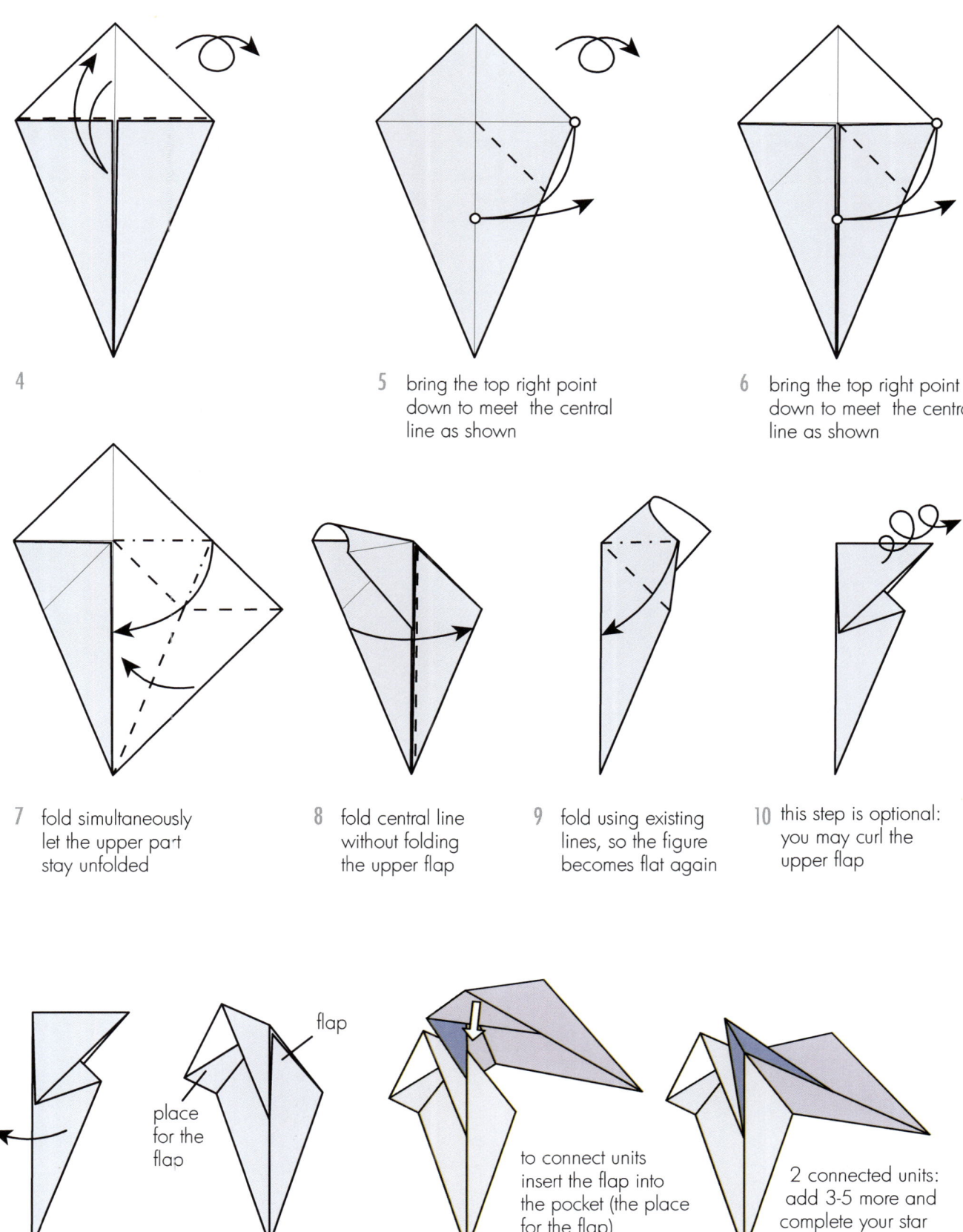

7x7 cm square

5-8 units

FLOWERET
VARIATIONS

Variation A

Variation B

Variation A

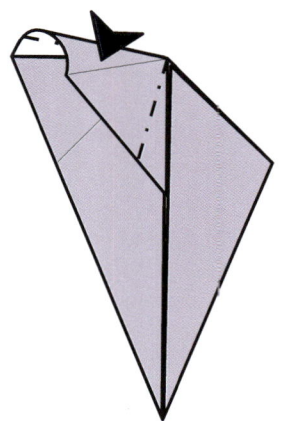 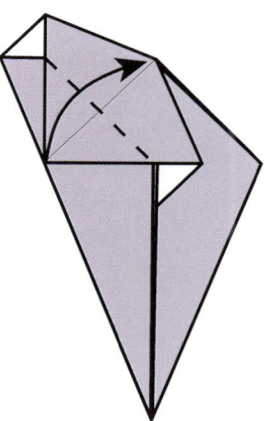 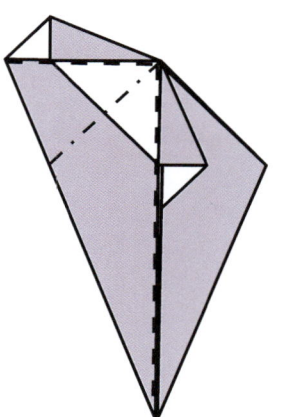 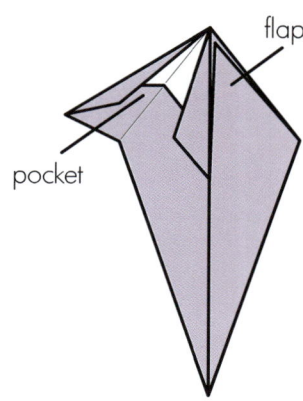

12 start with complete Floweret unit: squash the flap so that the central line lies on the line below, see next picture for reference

13

14 semi-fold along the marked lines

15 connect units the same way as Floweret

Variation B

11 start with step 11 of Floweret

12

13 squash fold

14

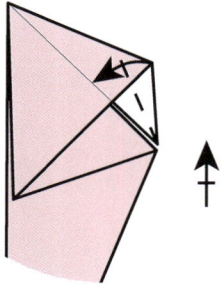 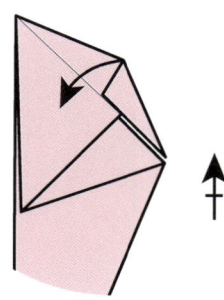 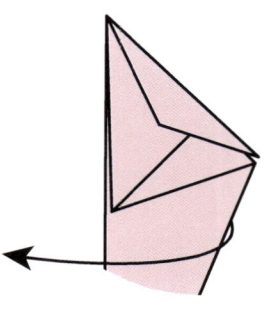 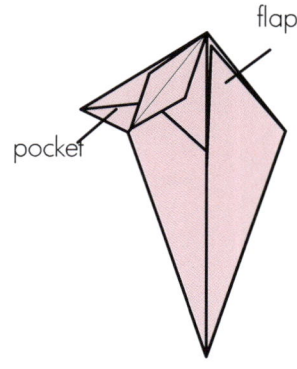

15 repeat step on the other side

16 repeat step on the other side

17 unfold a bit, next picture shows the whole unit

complete unit: connect the same way as Floweret units

23

5 units

7x7 cm square

COMPASS
STAR

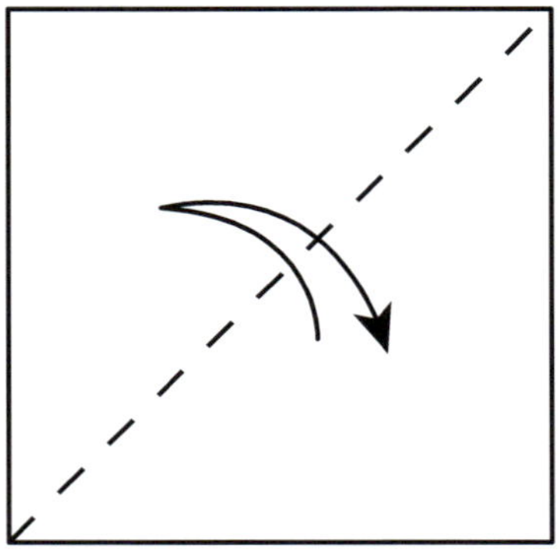

1

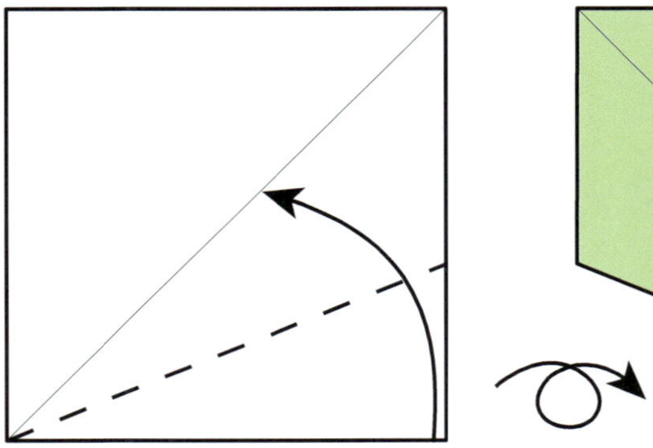

2

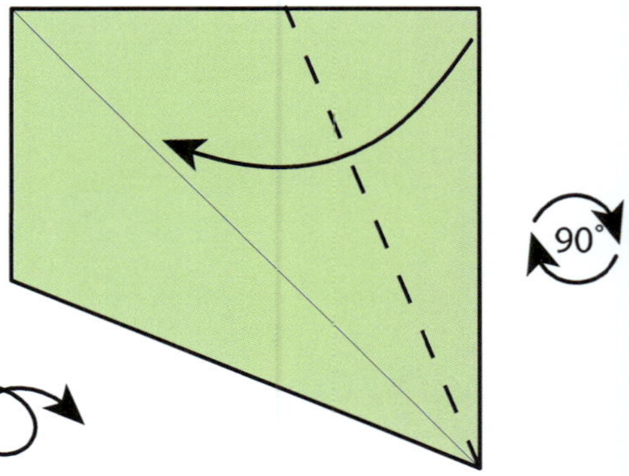

3

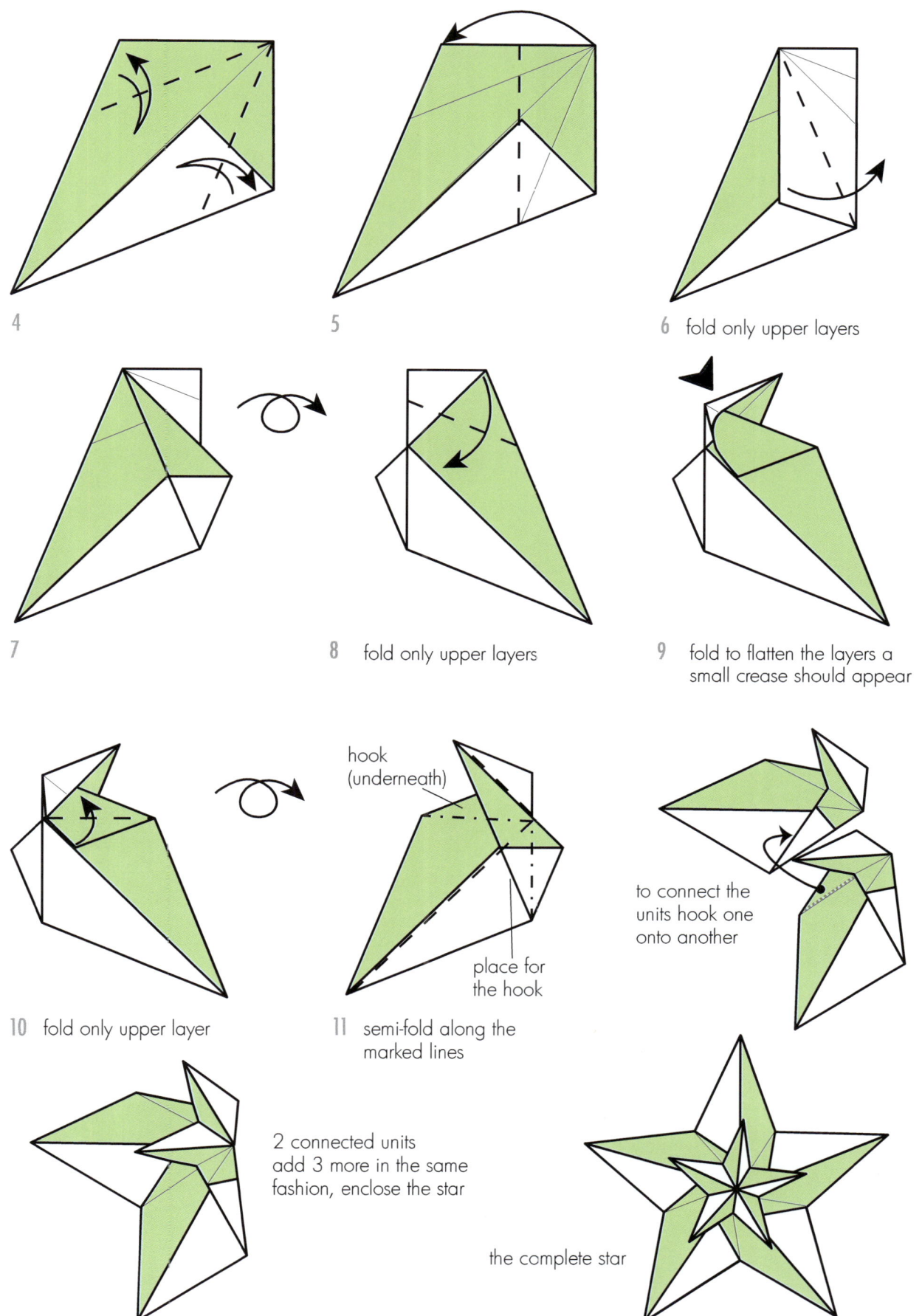

30A

7x7 cm square

RIO

This kusudama got its name after Rio-de-Janeiro, the city with splendid hills and forests.

30A

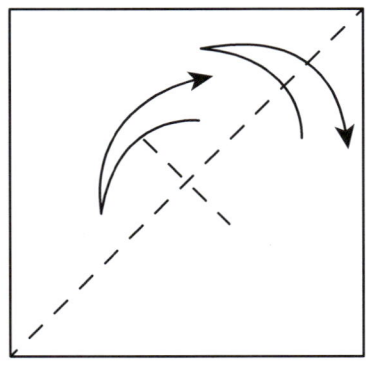

1

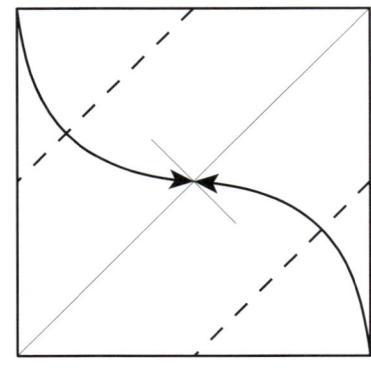

2

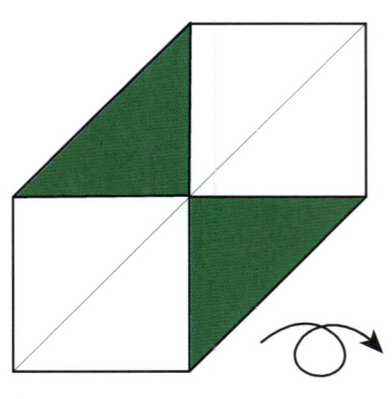

3

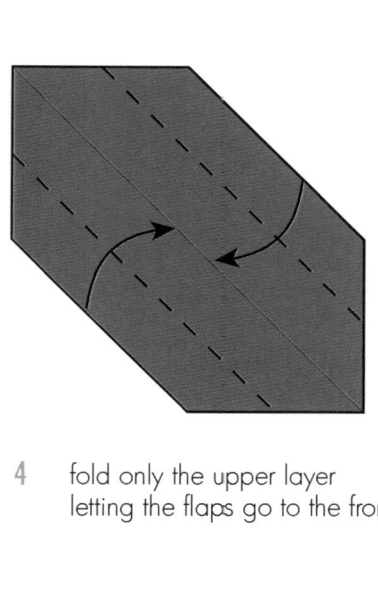

4 fold only the upper layer letting the flaps go to the front

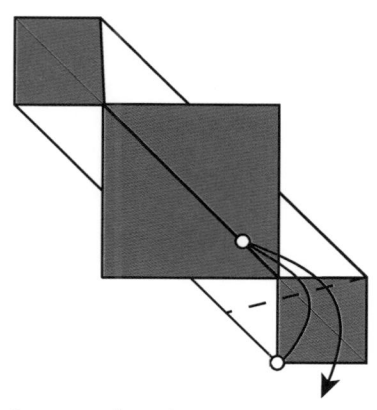

5 align the corner to the central line

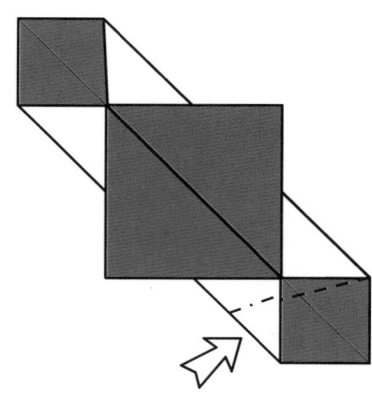

6 inside reverse fold

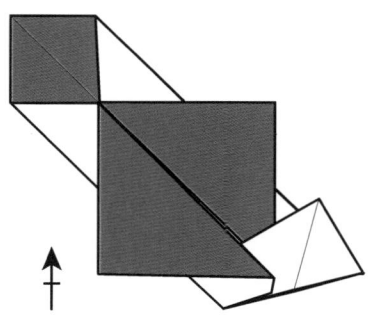

7 repeat steps 5-6 on the other side

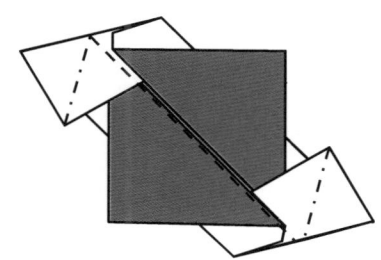

8 semi-fold along the marked lines

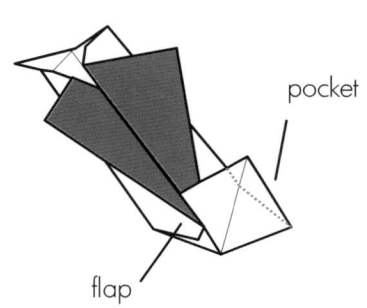

complete unit

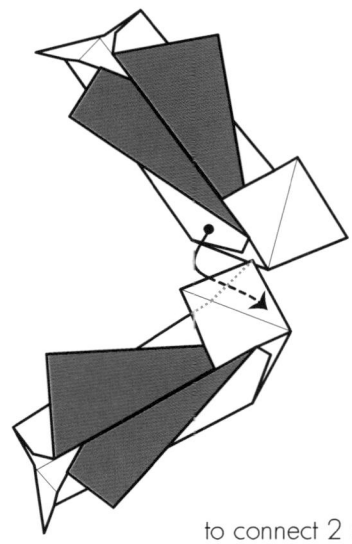

to connect 2 units together insert the flap into the pocket

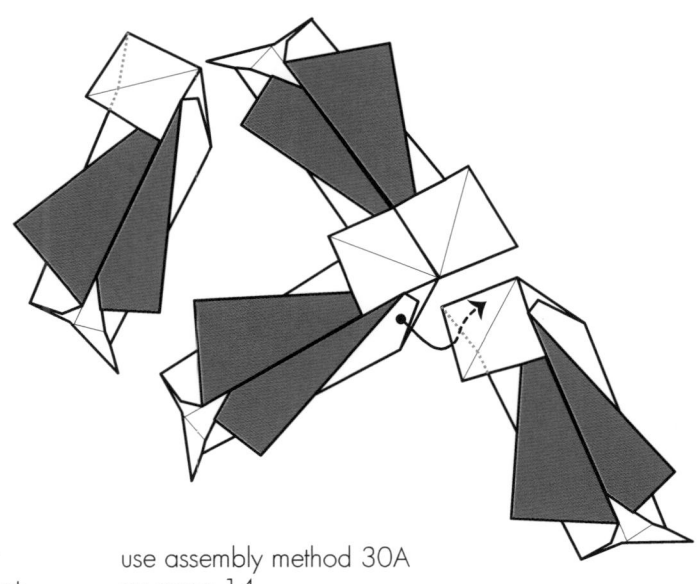

use assembly method 30A on page 14

30A, 12A

7x7 cm square

SERENADE

Curl the little loose flaps of this module to get a delicate look.

30A

12A

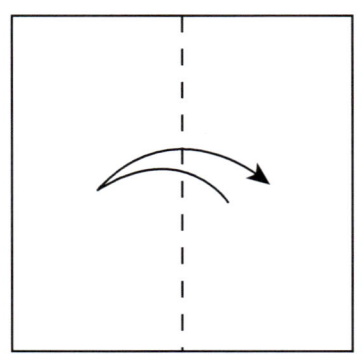

1

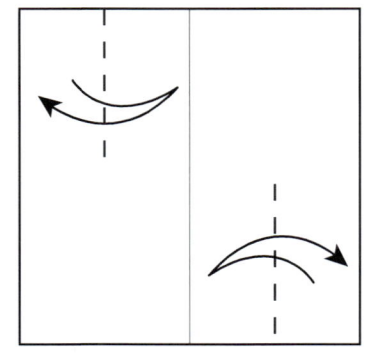

2

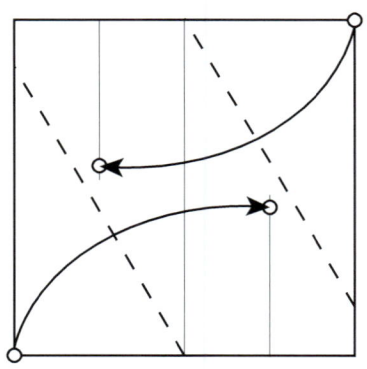

3 fold marked corners to the lines

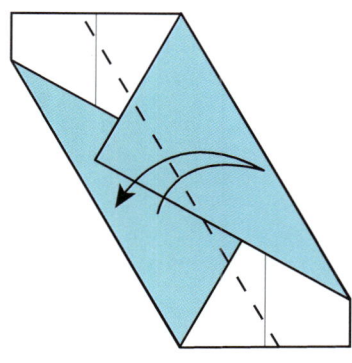

4

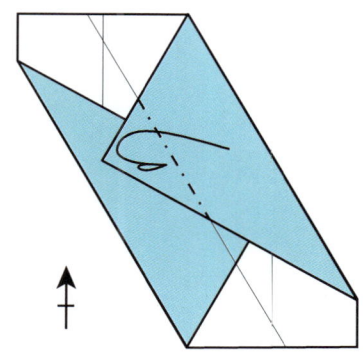

5 fold the little triangle under

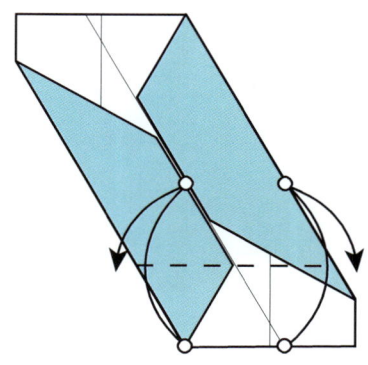

6 fold aligning the points

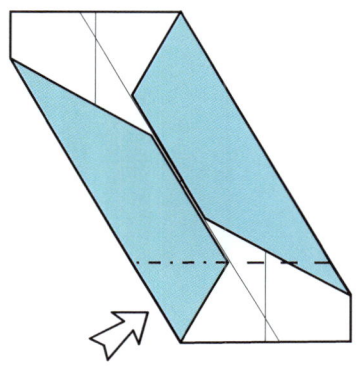

7 inside reverse fold

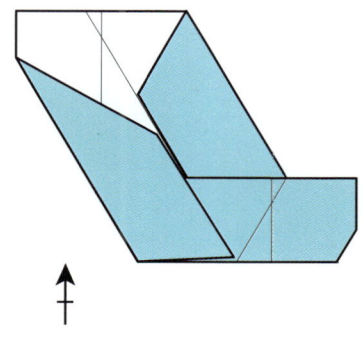

8 repeat steps 6-7 on the other side

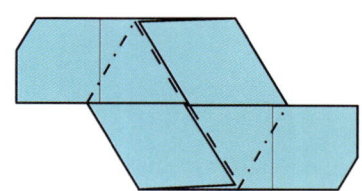

9 semi-fold along the marked lines

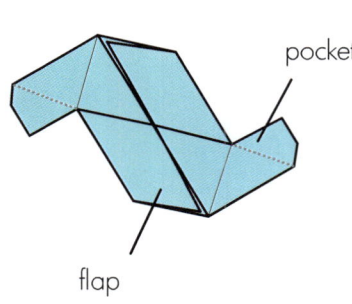

pocket

flap

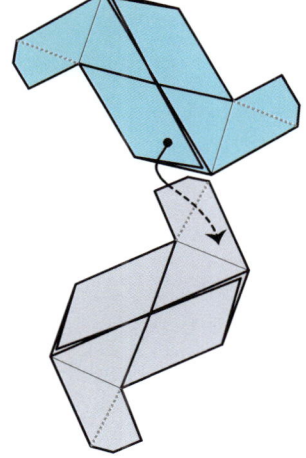

to connect 2 units together insert the flap into the pocket

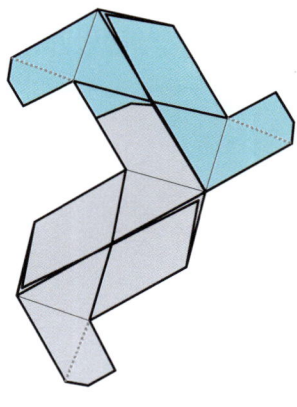

2 connected units
use assembly method 30A on page 14 or method 12A on page 12

29

 ★★
30A, 12A

6.1 x 7 cm rectangle (proportion 2 : √3 or 1:1.15)

JADE STAR

30A

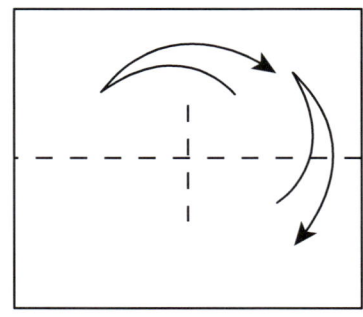

1 start with 2:√3 rectangle, see page 9 for the cutting instructions

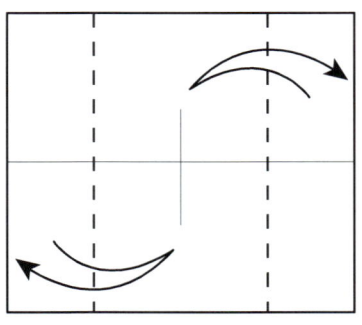

2

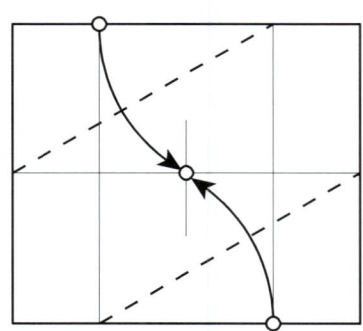

3 align points to the center

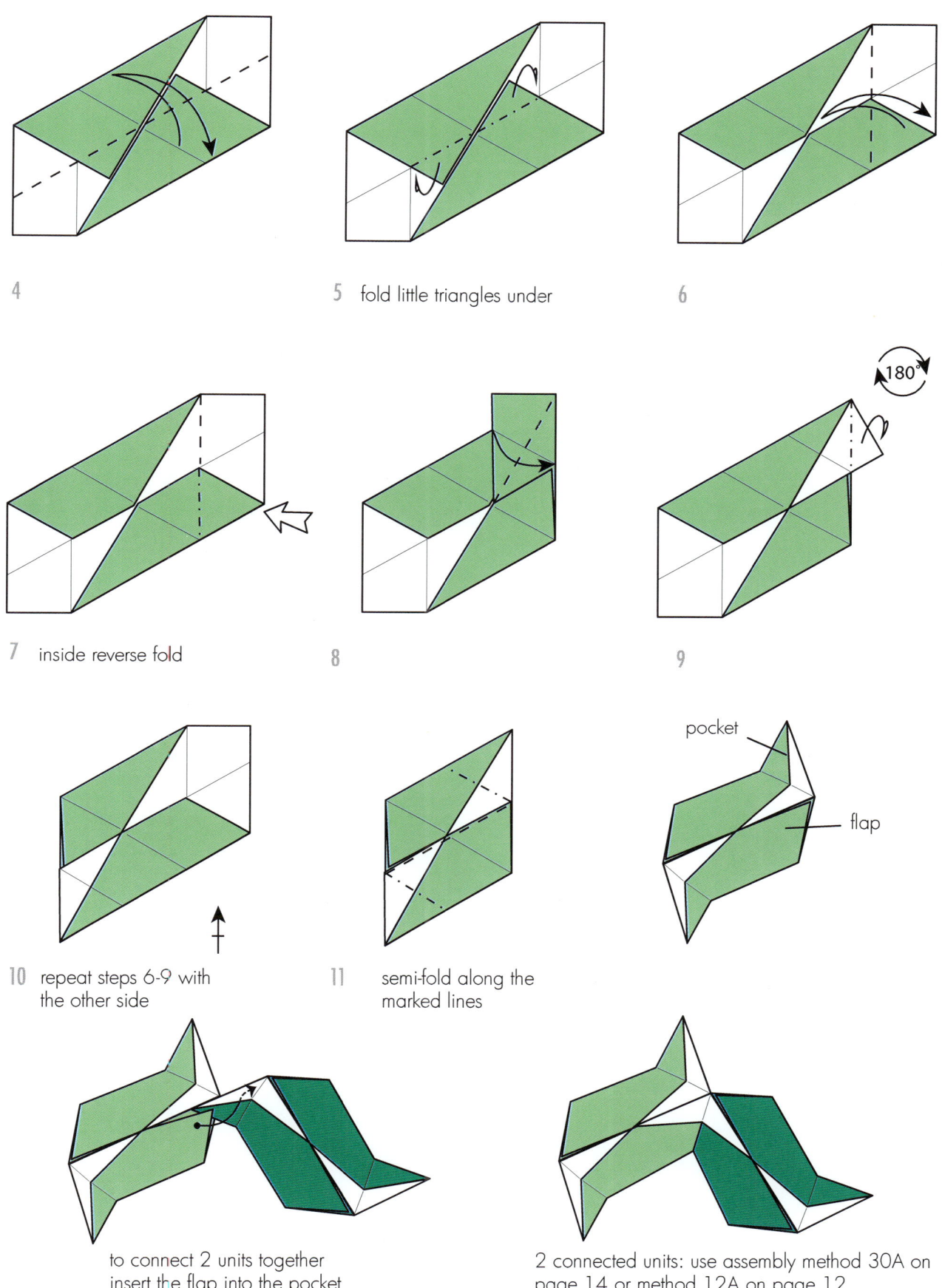

30A

7x7 cm square

CENTAUREA CYANUS

30A

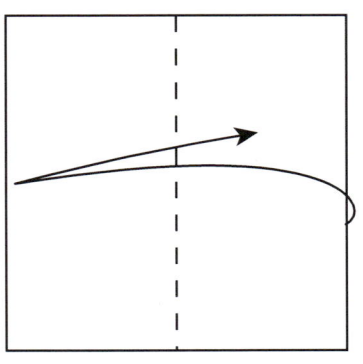

1

2 fold the corner to the line and unfold

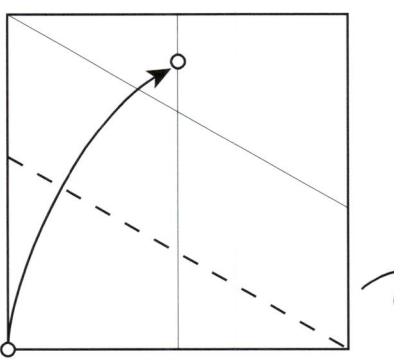

3 fold the corner to the line

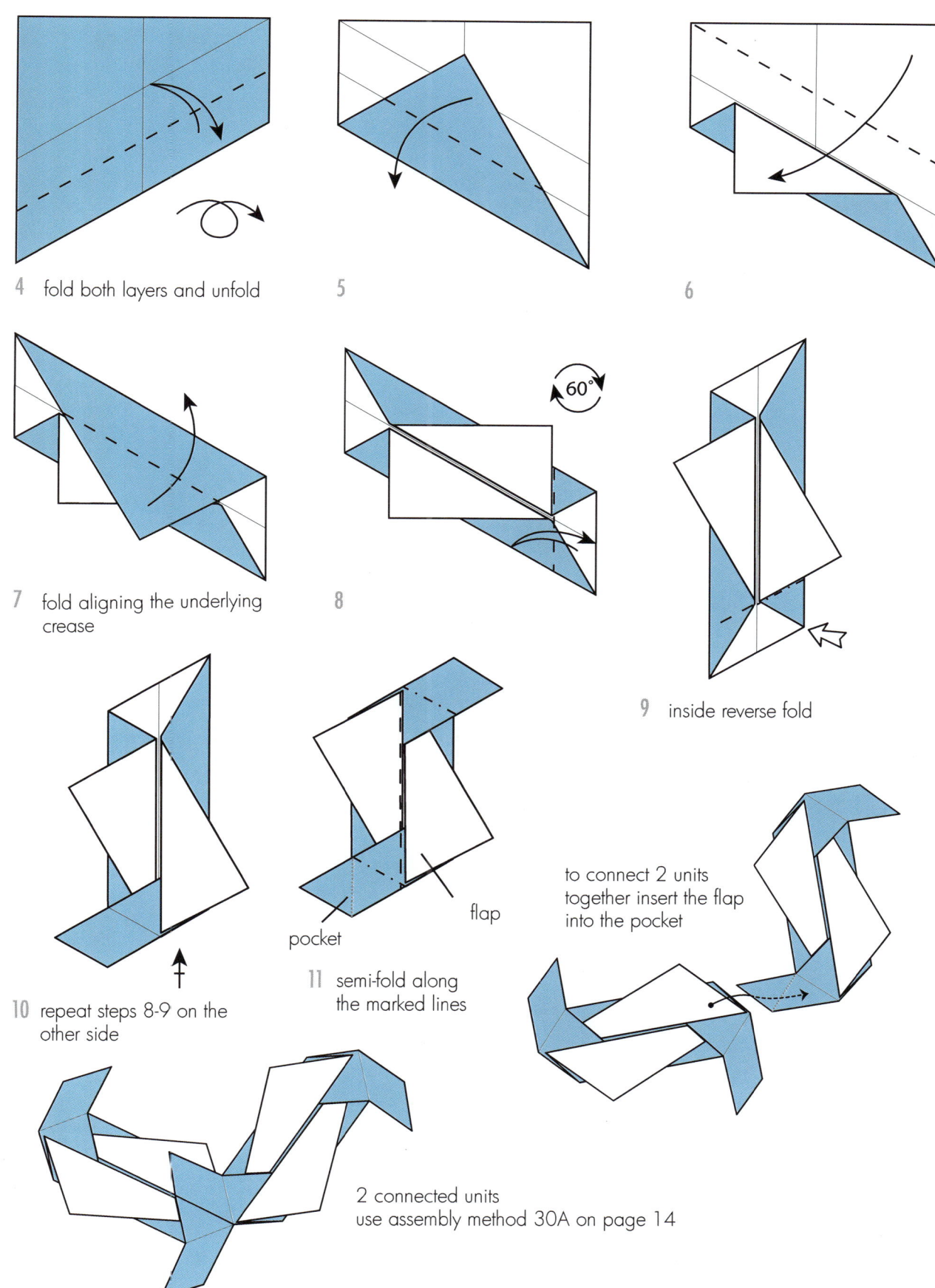

4 fold both layers and unfold

7 fold aligning the underlying crease

9 inside reverse fold

10 repeat steps 8-9 on the other side

11 semi-fold along the marked lines

pocket

flap

to connect 2 units together insert the flap into the pocket

2 connected units
use assembly method 30A on page 14

30A

7x7 cm square

CENTAUREA FLOWER

30A

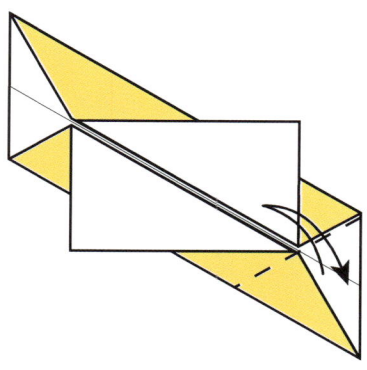

8 start with step 8 of Centaurea Cyanus model on page 32

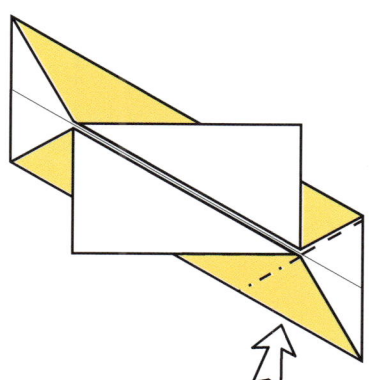

9 inside reverse fold

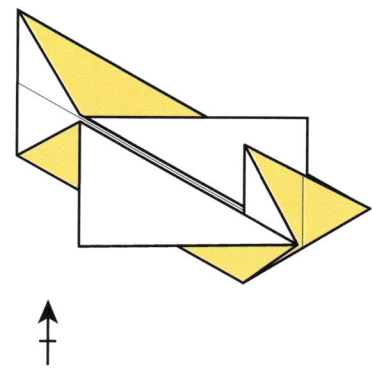

10 repeat steps 8-9 on the other side

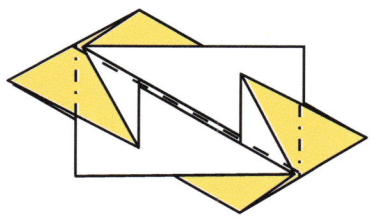

11 semi-fold along the marked lines

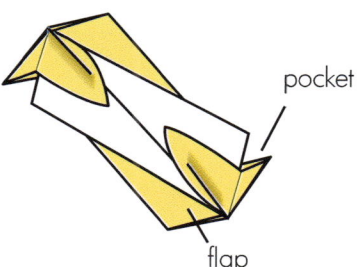

pocket

flap

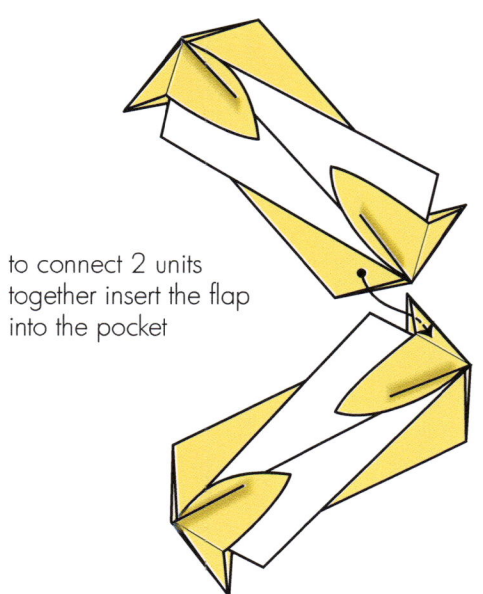

to connect 2 units together insert the flap into the pocket

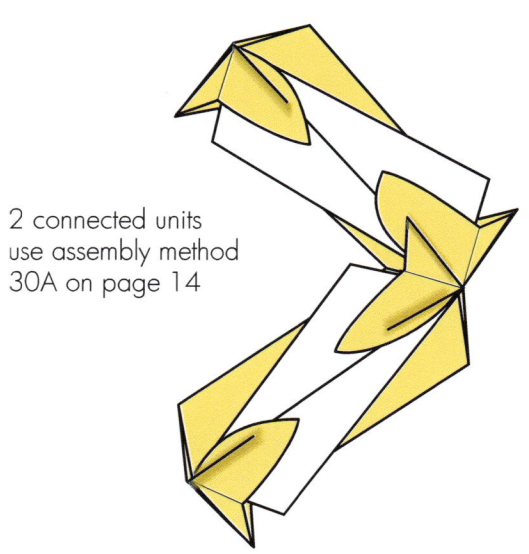

2 connected units use assembly method 30A on page 14

★★
30A, 12A

6 x 12 cm rectangle (proportion 1:2)

BOUQUET

30A

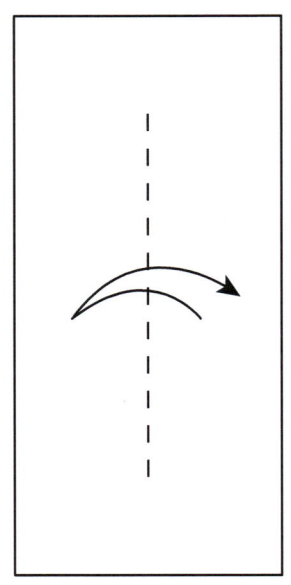

1 start with 1:2 rectangle, see page 8 for cutting instructions

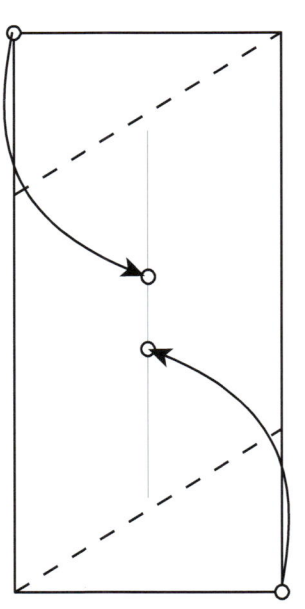

2 fold the marked corners to the line

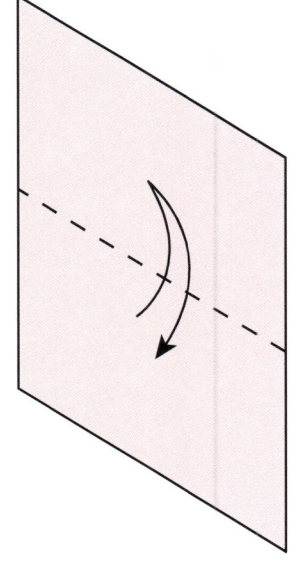

3

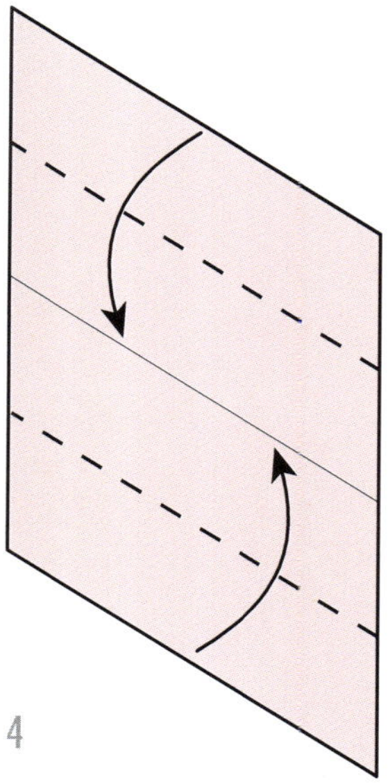

4

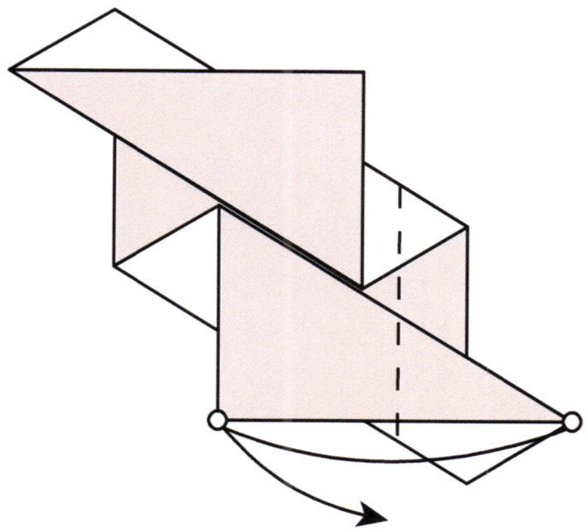

5

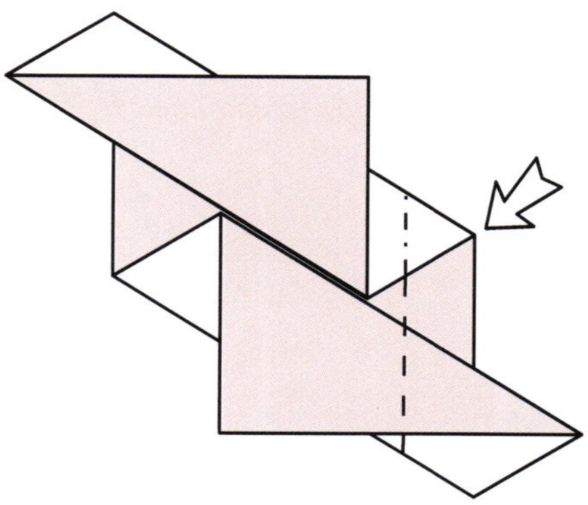

6 inside reverse fold

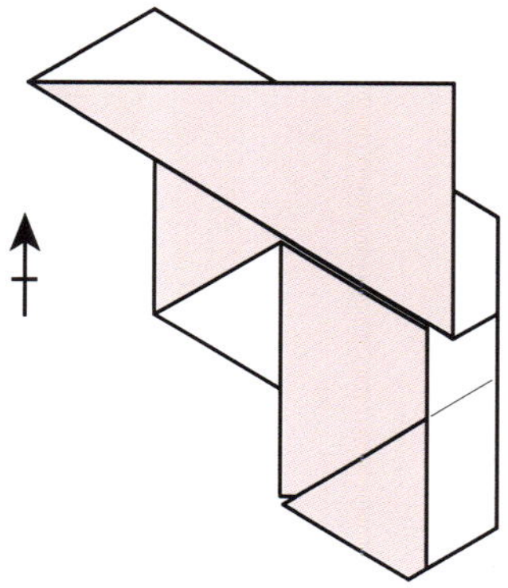

7 repeat the steps 5-6 with on the other side

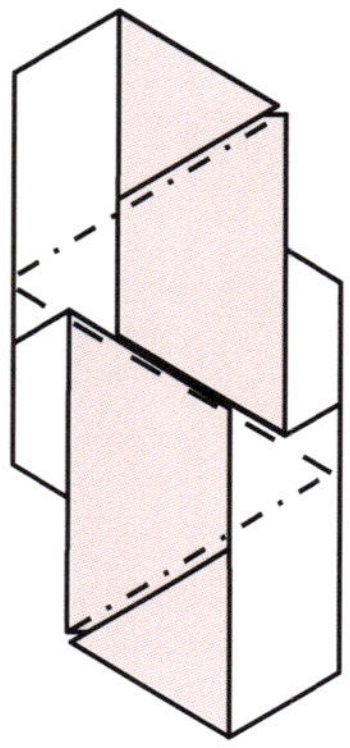

8 semi-fold along the marked lines

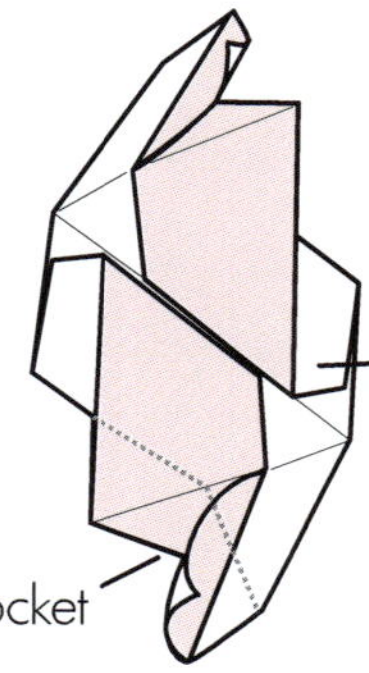

complete unit

flap

pocket

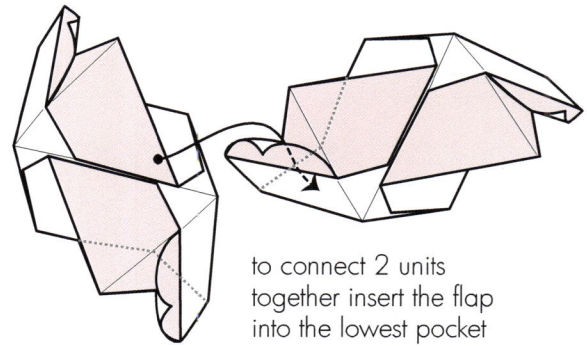

to connect 2 units together insert the flap into the lowest pocket

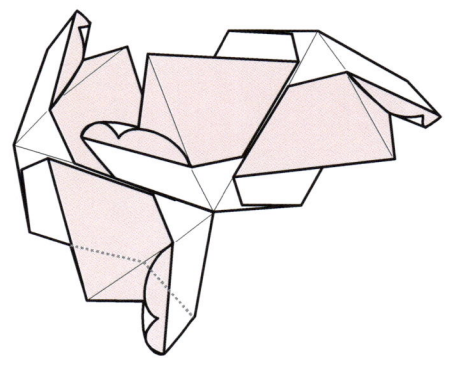

2 connected units
use assembly method 30A on page 14
or assembly method 12A on page 12

30A, 12A

6 x 12 cm rectangle (proportion 1:2)

DAISY BOUQUET

30A

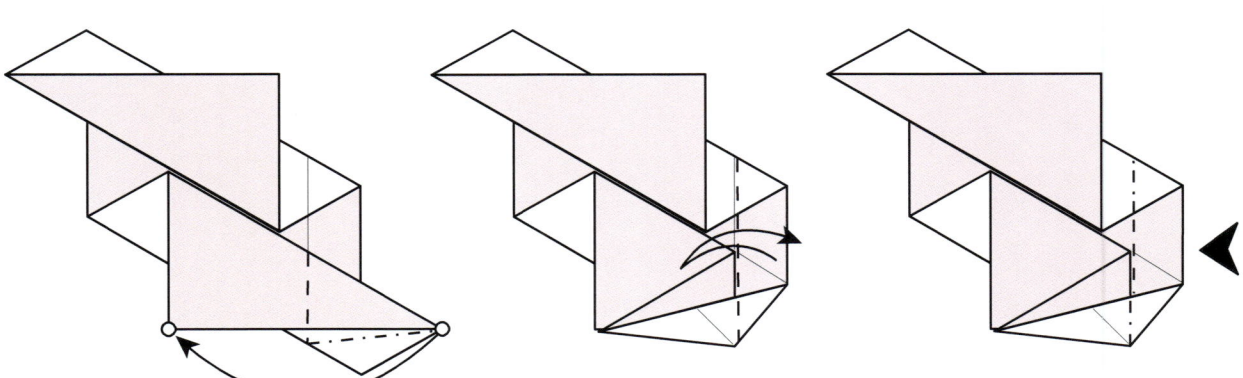

6   start with step 6 of Bouquet on page 36, align the points and make a crease so that the result is flat

7

8   sink fold both sides

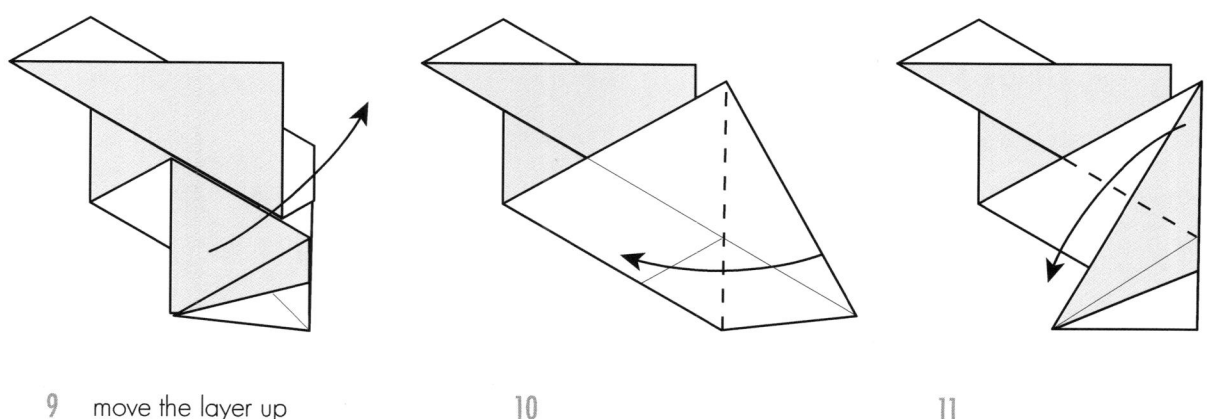

9 move the layer up

10

11

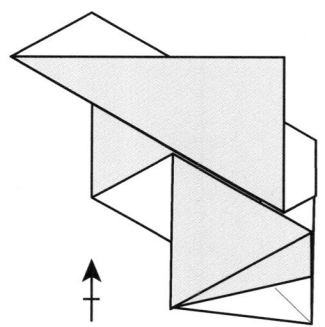

12 repeat steps 5-11 on the other side

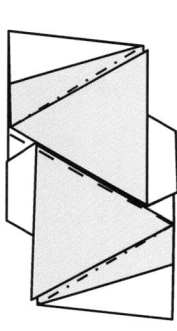

13 semi-fold along the marked lines

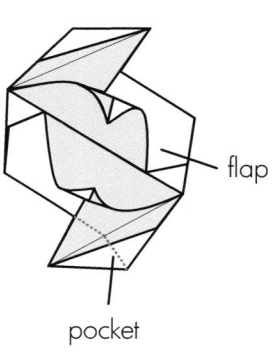

flap

pocket

complete unit

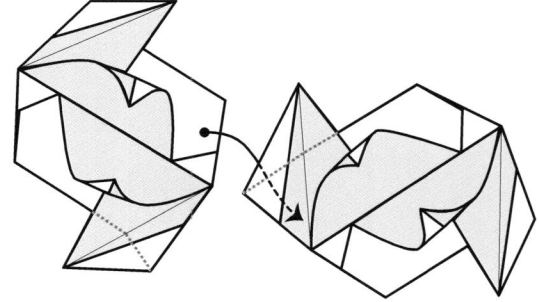

to connect 2 units together insert the flap into the pocket

2 connected units
use assembly method 30A on page 14
or assembly method 12A on page 12

39

30A, 30B, 12A, 12B

7 x 8 cm rectangle (proportion 2:√3 or 1:1.15)

ORNAMENTARIUM

30A

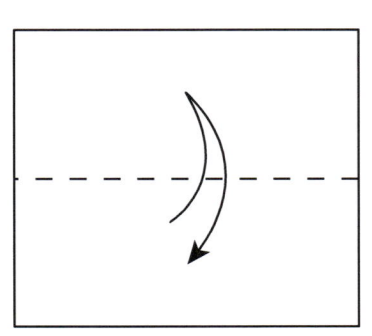

1 start with 2:√3 rectangle see page 9 for cutting instructions

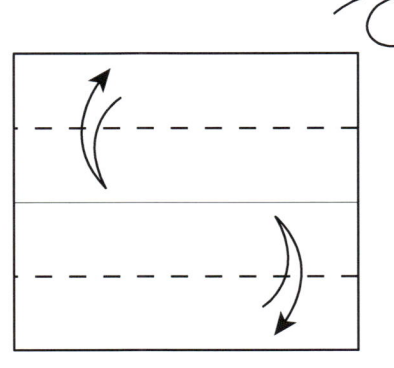

2

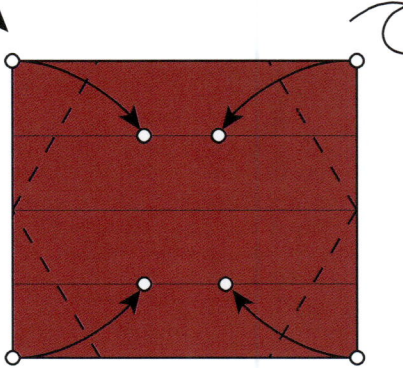

3 fold the corners to the lines

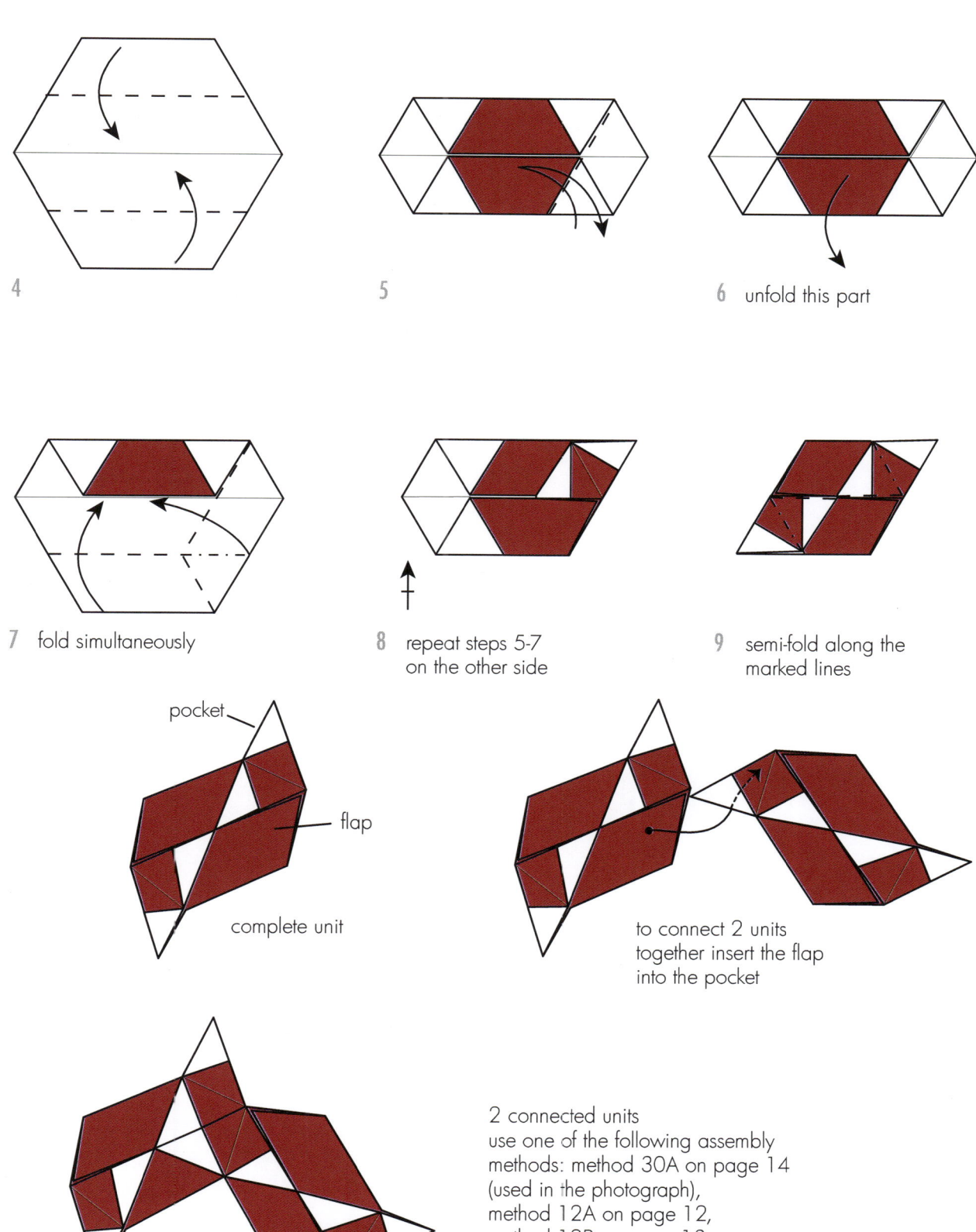

4

5

6 unfold this part

7 fold simultaneously

8 repeat steps 5-7 on the other side

9 semi-fold along the marked lines

pocket
flap
complete unit

to connect 2 units together insert the flap into the pocket

2 connected units
use one of the following assembly methods: method 30A on page 14 (used in the photograph), method 12A on page 12, method 12B on page 13, method 30B on page 15

30A, 30B, 12A, 12B

7 x N cm rectangle where N>8 (proportion 1:X, where X>1.15)

ORNAMENTARIUM
ANYSIZE

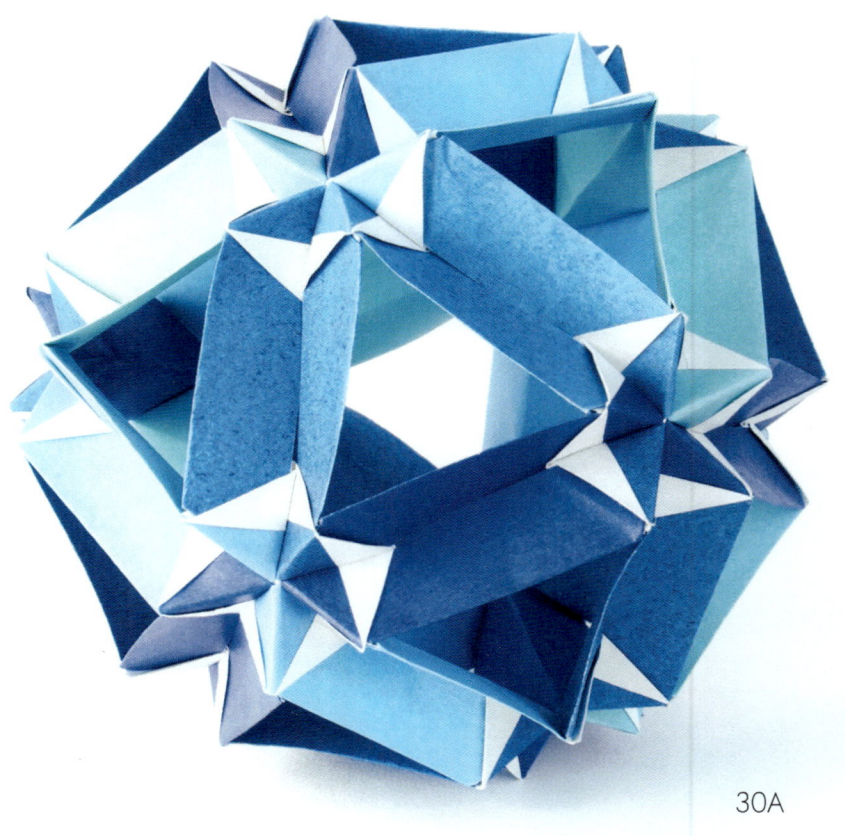

30A

use rectangles with the sides 1:X, where X>1.15. Do all the steps of Ornamentarium on page 40 with this longer rectangle

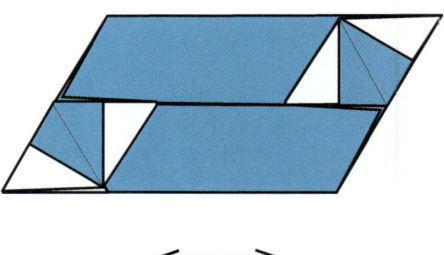

the longer the initial rectangle is the longer is the space between decorative parts of the complete unit, the size of the gap equals B — 1.15A, where A x B is the side of an initial rectangle

connect the units the same way as Ornamentarium units

30A, 12B

7x7 square

PHOENIX

30A

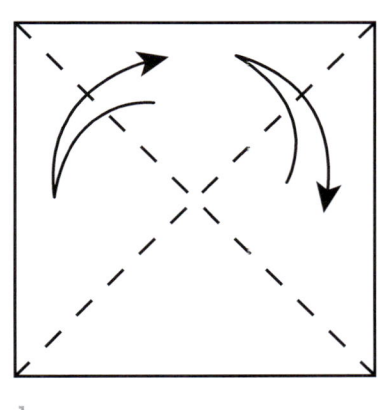

1

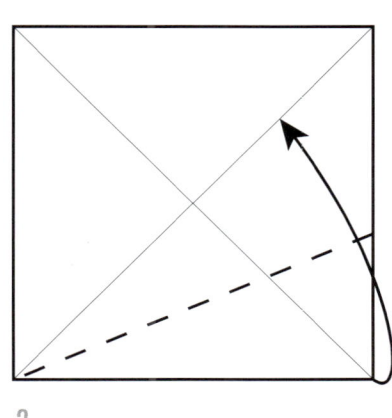

2

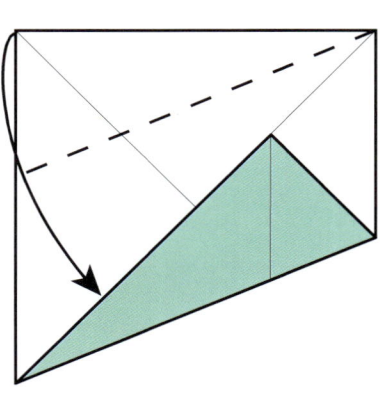

3

43

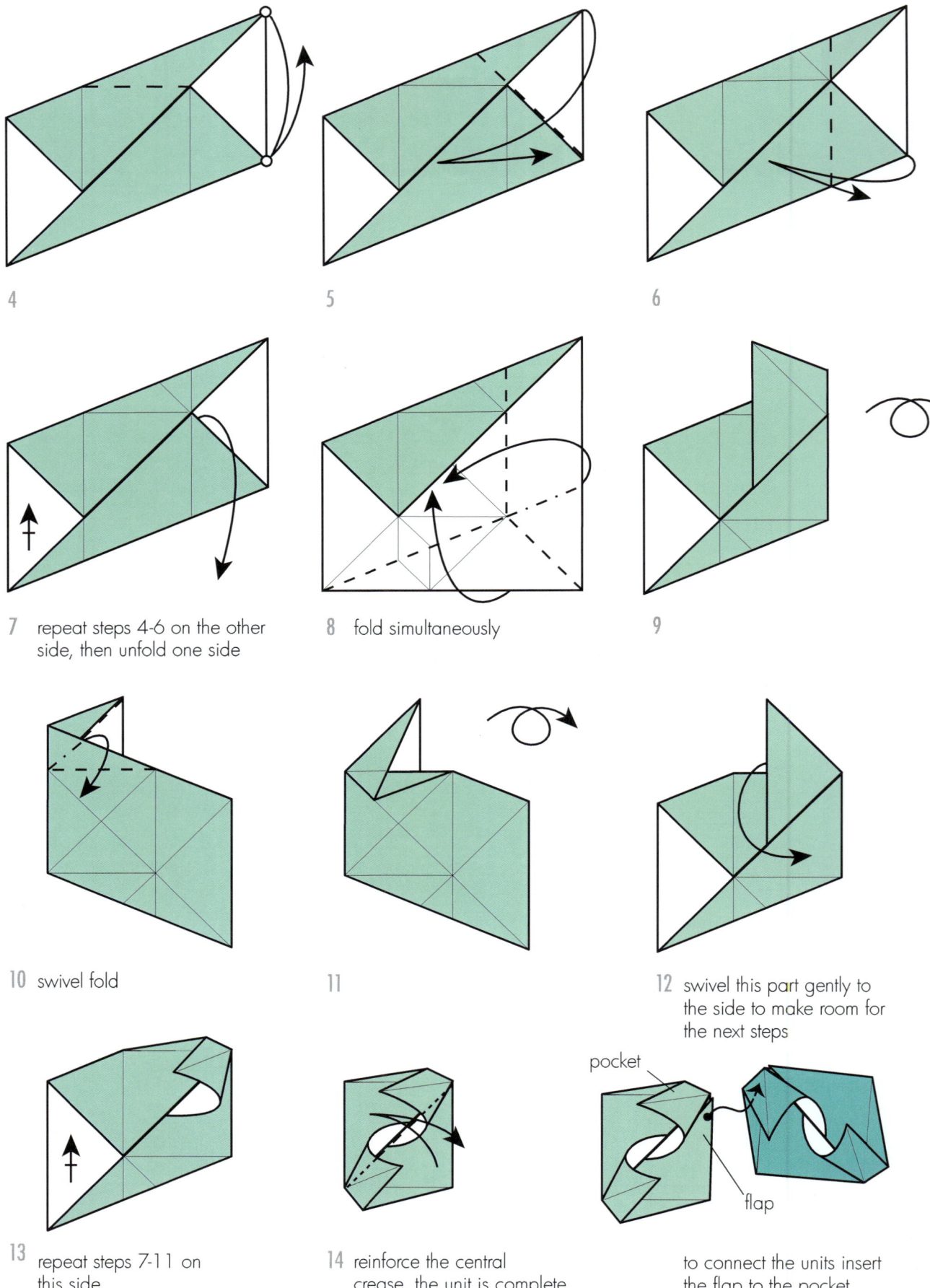

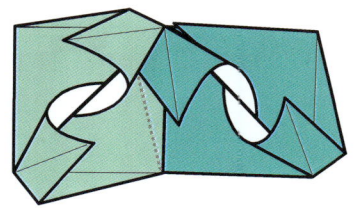

2 connected units
see assembly method 30A on page 14, use assembly hint on page 16 to ease the process

☆☆☆
30A, 12B

7 x 7 cm square

PHOENIX
FEATHER

This is a lightweight version of Phoenix. It may seem like nothing will hold this ball together, but with experience and good crisp paper, you can assemble it without any glue. If you are novice to modular origami, don't hesitate to use glue.

30A

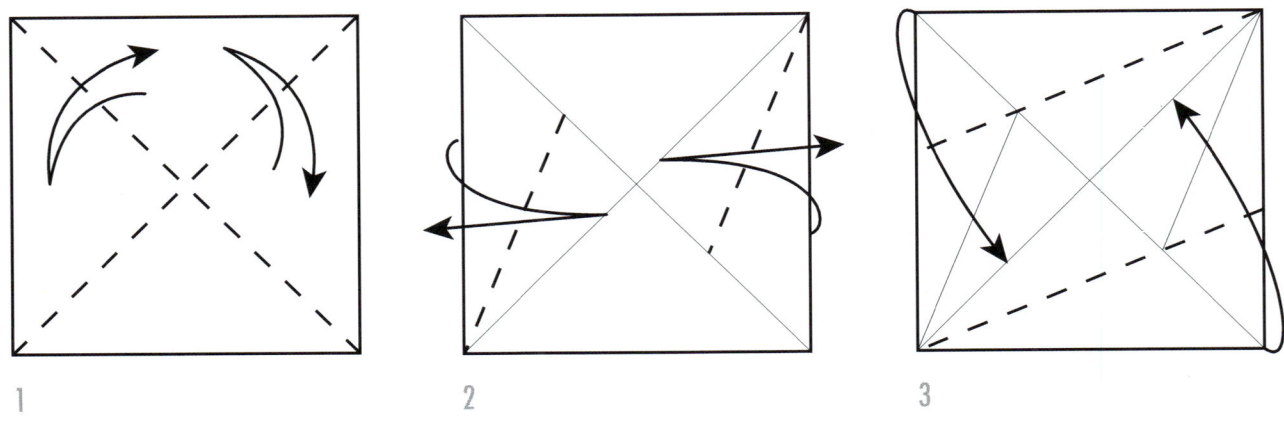

1

2

3

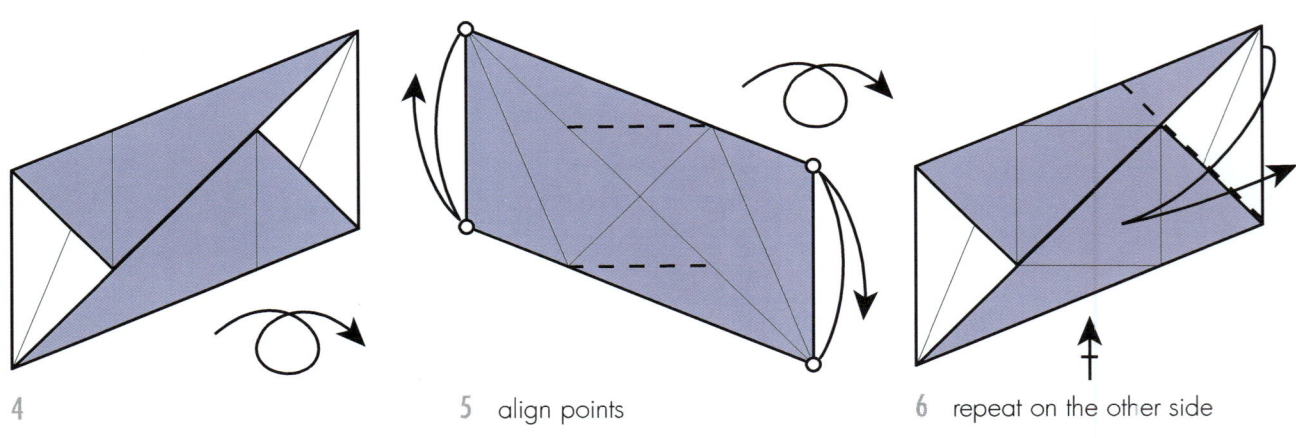

4

5 align points

6 repeat on the other side

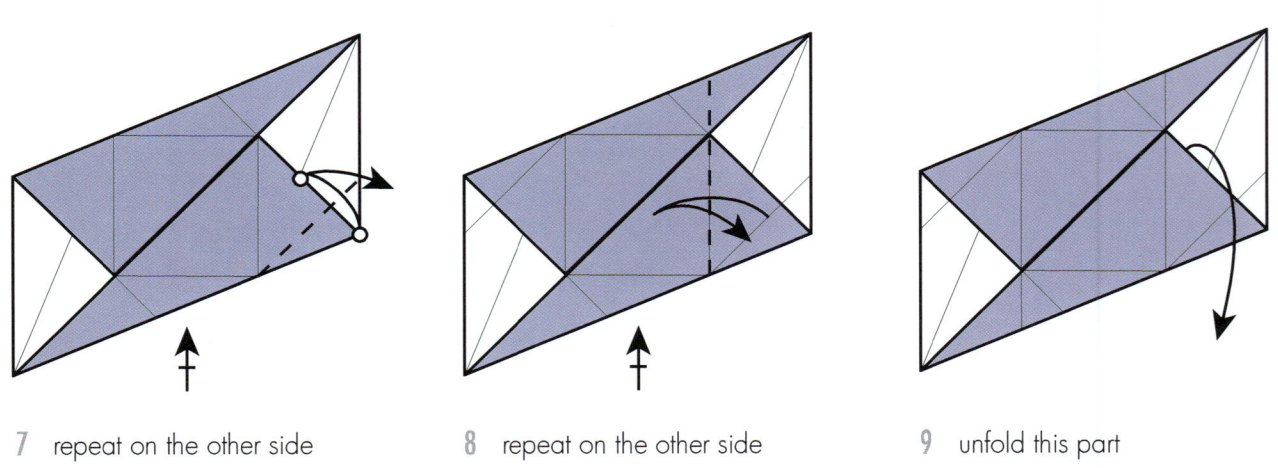

7 repeat on the other side

8 repeat on the other side

9 unfold this part

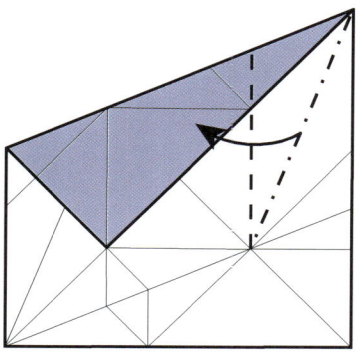

10 fold simultaneously, part of the unit will pop up

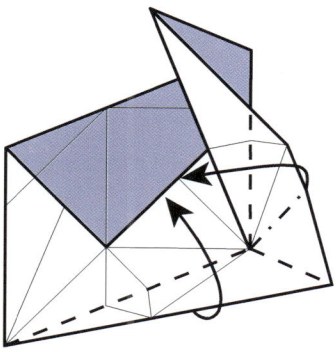

11 flatten the figure using the marked lines

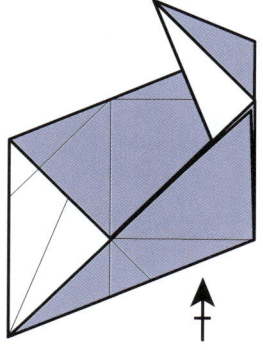

12 repeat steps 9-11 on the other side

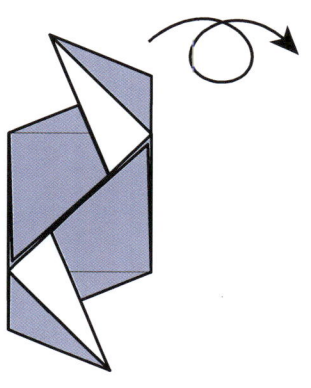

13

14 swivel fold

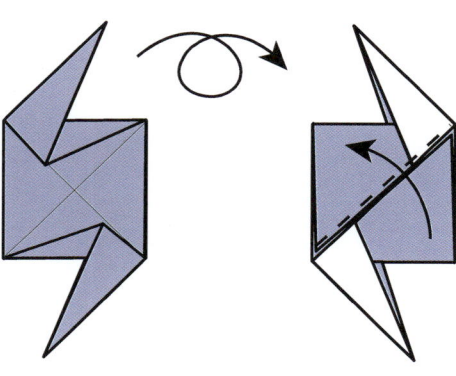

15

16 reinforce the central crease

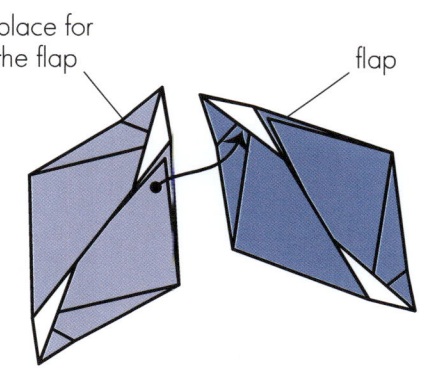

to connect 2 units put the flap into the place for the flap

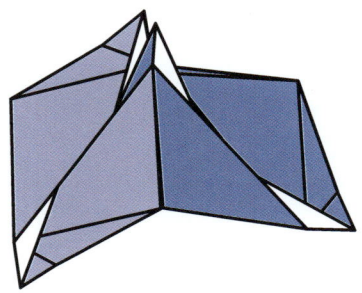

2 connected units
use assembly method 30A on page 14 or assembly method 12A on page 12, use assembly hint on page 16 to ease the process

 30A, 12A

7x7 cm square

MALACHITE

This easy unit is extremely versatile and, with a slight change in folding procedure, you can perform a lot of different ornamental designs. Create your very own malachite ball.

30A

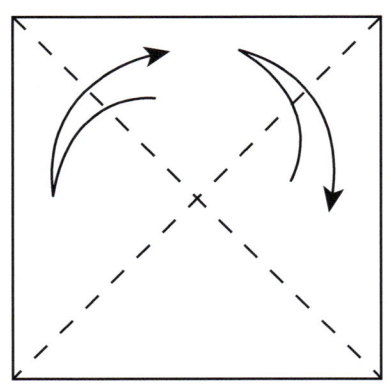

1

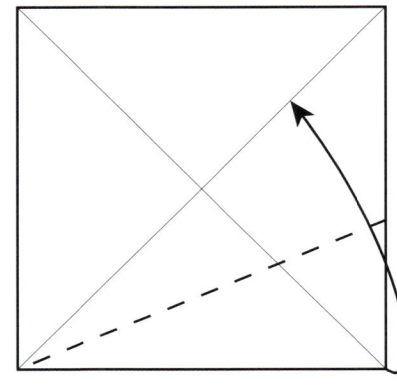

2

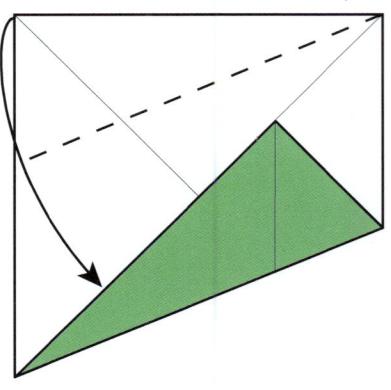

3

There are several possible variants for the next step, each variant will lead to a different coloring scheme in the end. The diagrams proceed for variant a, if you choose b or c, proceed to step 5 keeping in mind that the diagrams won't match your module completely, especially in color distribution. You can watch the difference this step brings to the model in the next few pages.

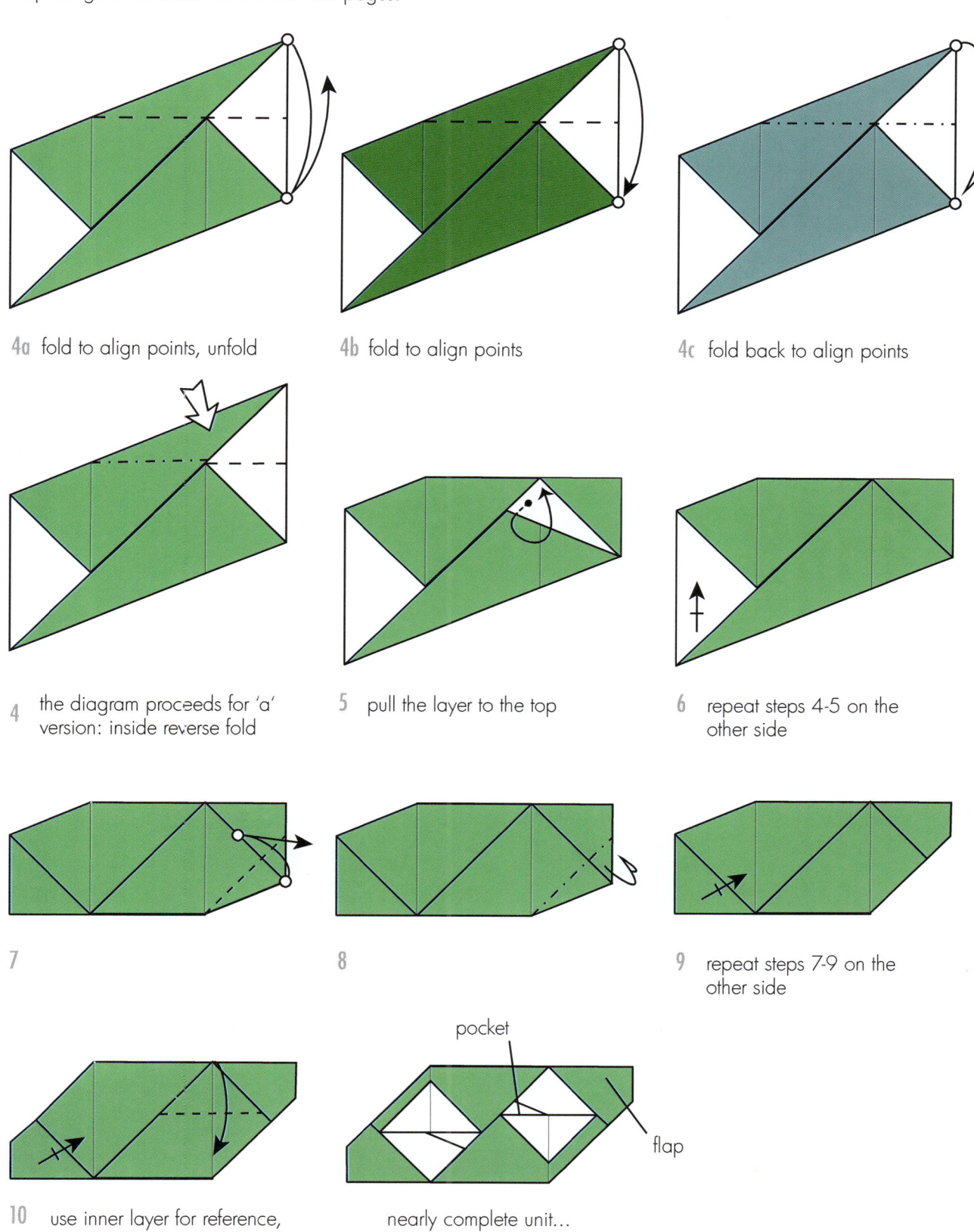

4a fold to align points, unfold

4b fold to align points

4c fold back to align points

4 the diagram proceeds for 'a' version: inside reverse fold

5 pull the layer to the top

6 repeat steps 4-5 on the other side

7

8

9 repeat steps 7-9 on the other side

10 use inner layer for reference, repeat on the other side

nearly complete unit...

pocket

flap

49

There are two different ways to use the same unit. Depending on how you pre-crease the unit before the assembly the ornament on the surface of the modular ball will be completely different. Units of type II hold together a bit stronger than units of type I. If you try different ways to perform step 4 of the Malachite diagram and combine it with different types of unit pre-creasing you can get numerous color ornaments out of nearly the same unit. Give it a try and find your favorite ornament!

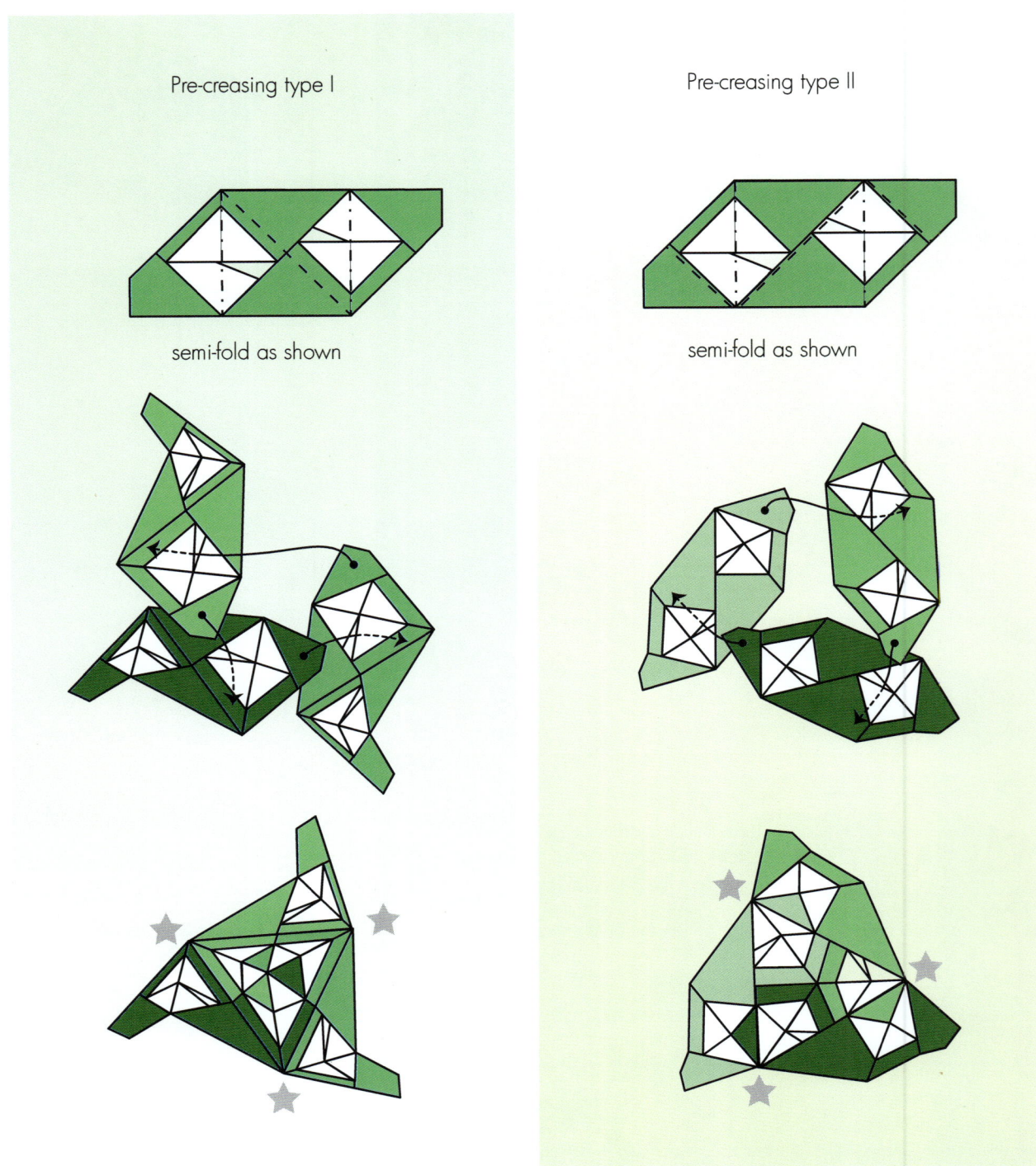

Connect units so that 4 (assembly method 12A on page 12) or 5 units (assembly method 30A on page 14) meet at the points marked with the stars in the picture.

The following illustrations represent the combination various 4th steps of Malachite diagram with different pre-crease methods. Three ways you variate the unit at 4th step and two types of unit pre-crease gives you 6 different patterns!

FLOWER VARIATION

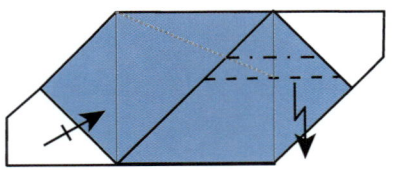

start with step 10 of Malachite type C
repeat step on both sides

10

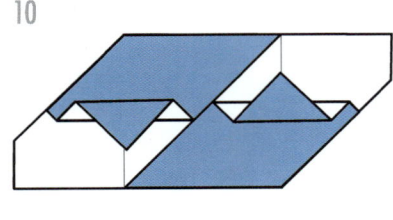

pre-crease type II to get the result in the picture

11

STAR VARIATION

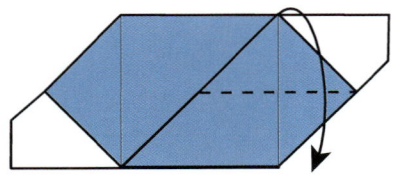 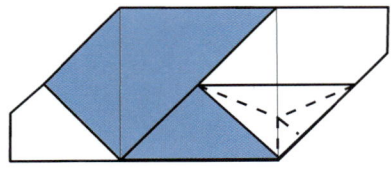 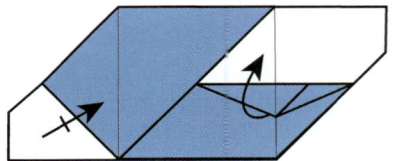

10 start with step 10 of Malachite type A or C

11 the diagram shows process for type C unit: rabbit ear fold

12 repeat steps 10-12 with the other side

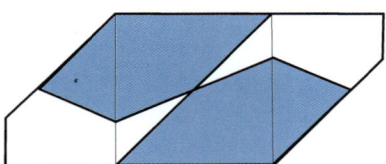

13 nearly complete unit semi-fold and assemble as type II to get the result in the picture

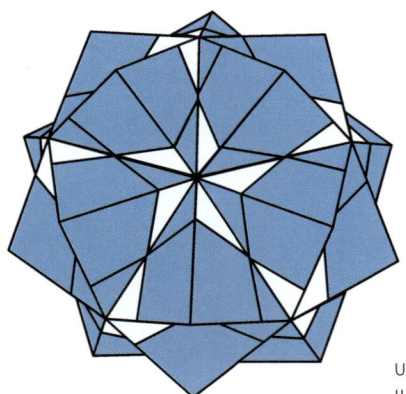

unit type A
II pre-crease type

unit type C
II pre-crease type

52

ORNAMENT VARIATION

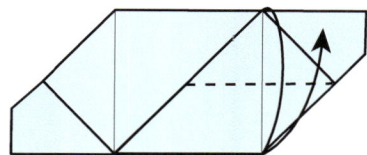 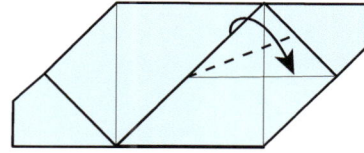 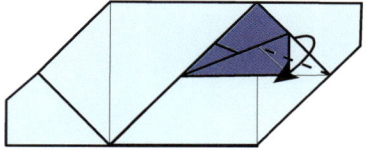

10 start with step 10 of Malachite type A

11

12

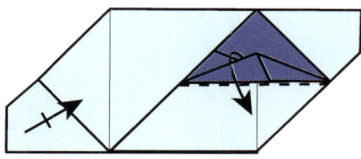 

13 repeat steps 10-12 with the other side

14 nearly complete unit semi-fold and assemble as type II to get the result in the pictures

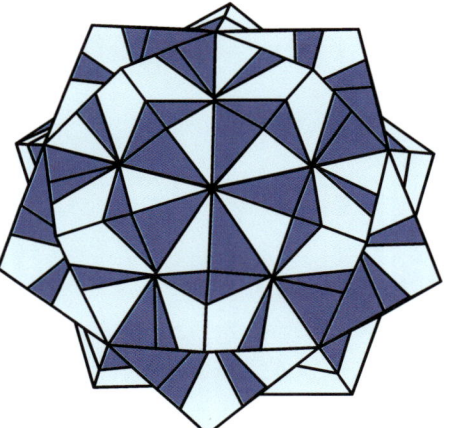

unit type A
I pre-crease type

unit type A
II pre-crease type

7x7 cm square

COMPASS
CUBE

This spectacular cube is fast to make. The tricky assembly process can be helped along with the assistance of paper clips placed in the recommended places. Once the cube is finished and the clips are removed, it will be quite stable.

12B

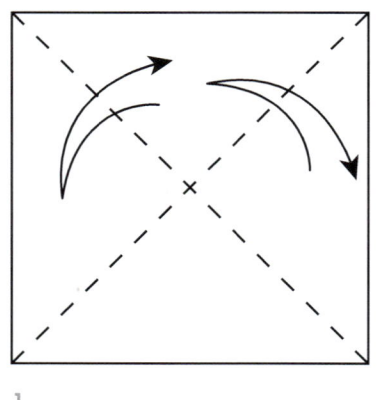

1

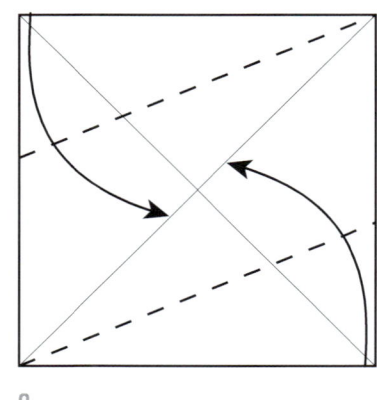

2

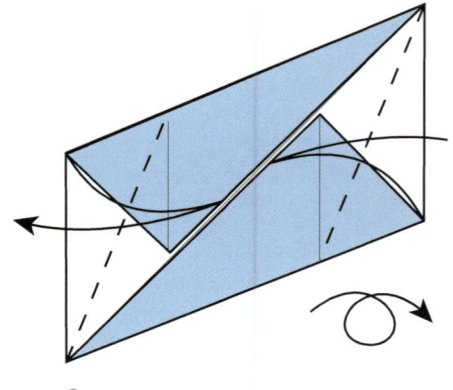

3

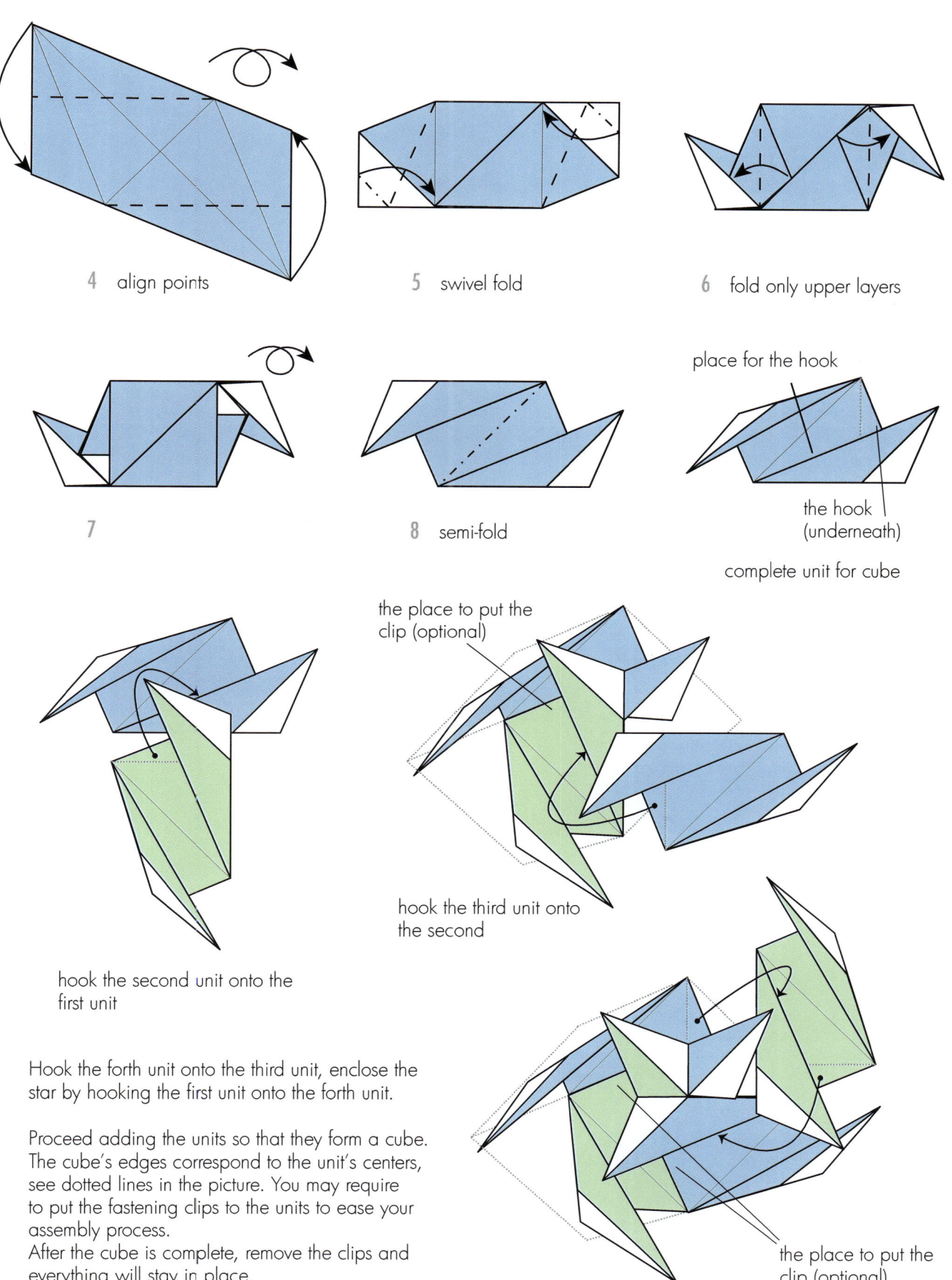

4 align points

5 swivel fold

6 fold only upper layers

7

8 semi-fold

place for the hook

the hook (underneath)

complete unit for cube

hook the second unit onto the first unit

the place to put the clip (optional)

hook the third unit onto the second

Hook the forth unit onto the third unit, enclose the star by hooking the first unit onto the forth unit.

Proceed adding the units so that they form a cube. The cube's edges correspond to the unit's centers, see dotted lines in the picture. You may require to put the fastening clips to the units to ease your assembly process.
After the cube is complete, remove the clips and everything will stay in place.

the place to put the clip (optional)

★★★
30A

7x7 cm square

COMPASS
BALL

This model uses nearly the same units as the Compass Cube model on previous pages. The only difference is that you pre-crease the units in a different manner and use a different assembly method. This model is more stable than Compass Cube during the assembly process.

30A

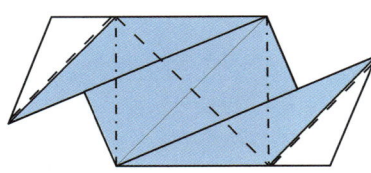

8 start with step 8 of Compass cube diagram on page 54, semi-fold the marked lines

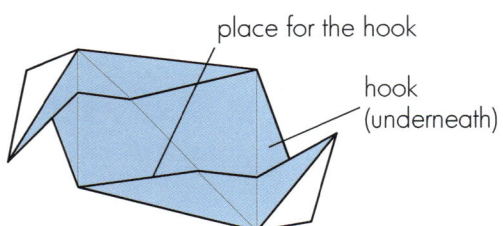

place for the hook

hook (underneath)

Compass ball module is complete

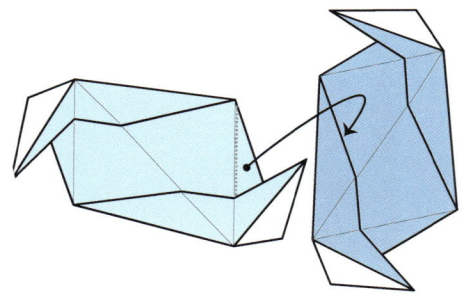

to connect units hook one onto another as shown

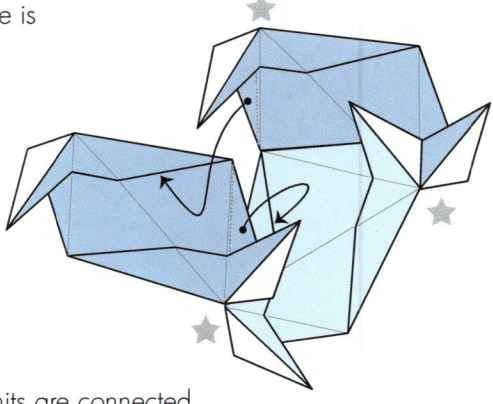

2 units are connected, add the third one to finish the pyramid, refer to assembly scheme 30A on page 14: each star in the picture corresponds to five units meeting at one point

30A, 12B

5x10 cm rectangle (proportion 1:2)

APRICOT

This module can be assembled both like a cube or like a ball.

30A

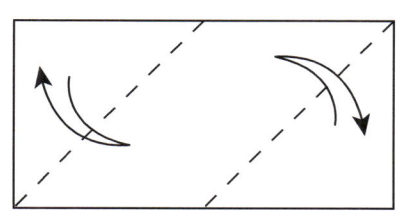

1 start with 1:2 rectangle paper
see page 8 for cutting instructions

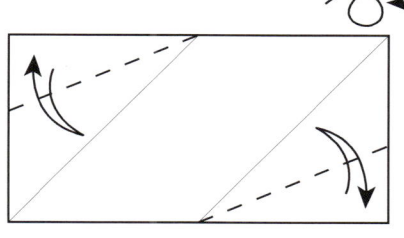

2

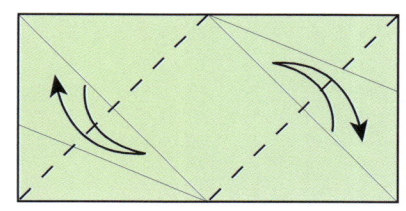

3

57

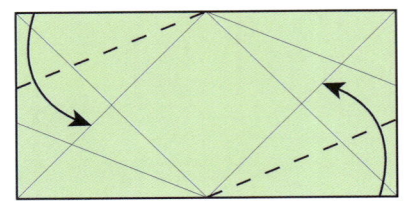

4

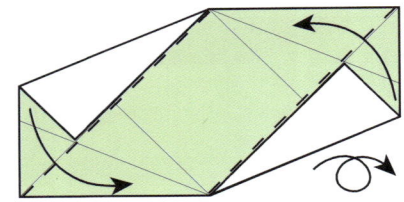

5

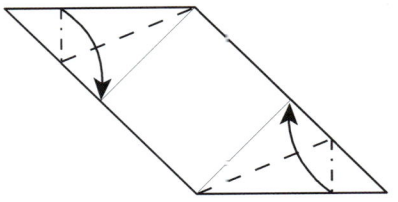

6 swivel fold

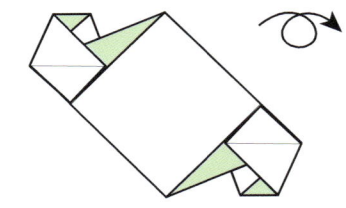

7

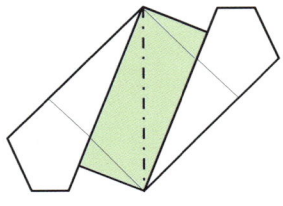

8a semi-fold: this is the unit for cube see Compass Cube on page 54 for assembly instructions

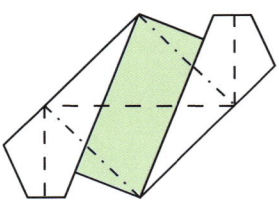

8b semi-fold along the marked lines to get the unit for the ball

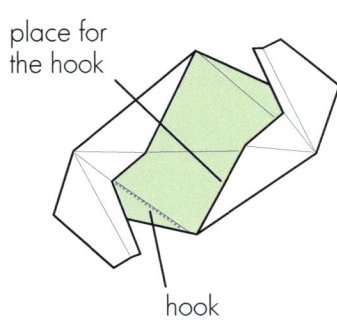

place for the hook

hook

this is the unit for ball, use assembly method 30A on page 14

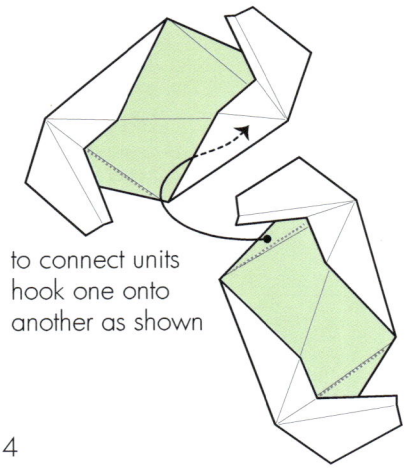

to connect units hook one onto another as shown

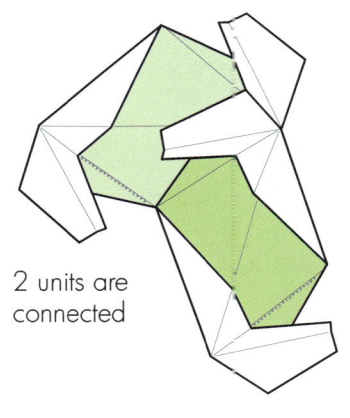

2 units are connected

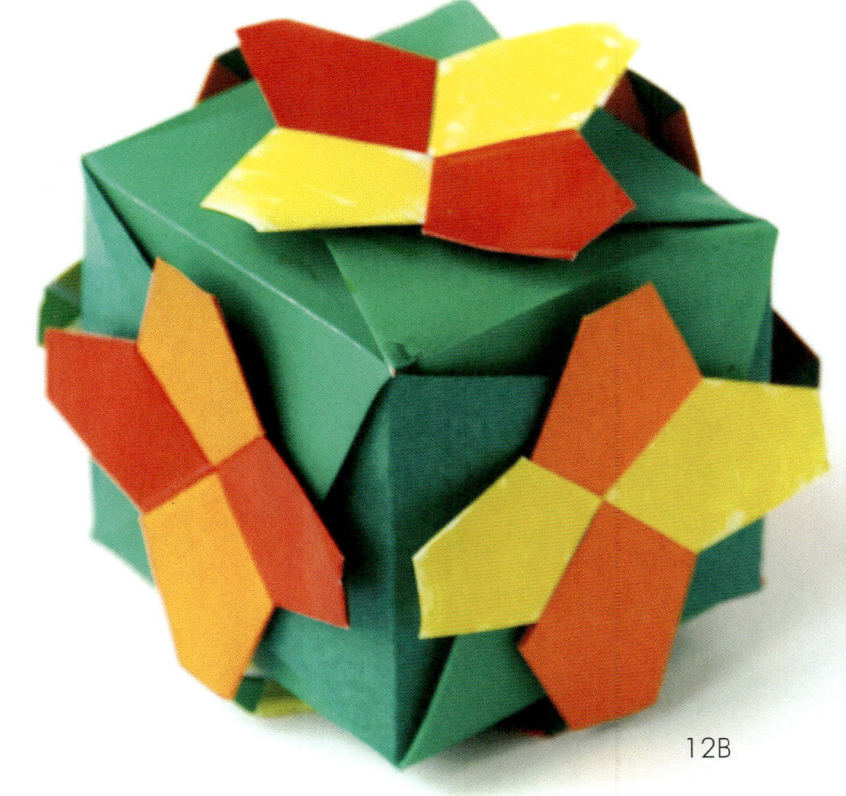

12B

★★★
30A, 12A

6x9 cm rectangle (proportion 2:3)

CELESTINA
FLOWER VARIATION

This kusudama has several variations. You can make it very serious, contemporary and urban if you use metallic colors for the Star variation. If you are in different mood, you can make it ornamental or flower style. Use pincer to curl petals, if you want it make your flower kusudama nicer.

30A

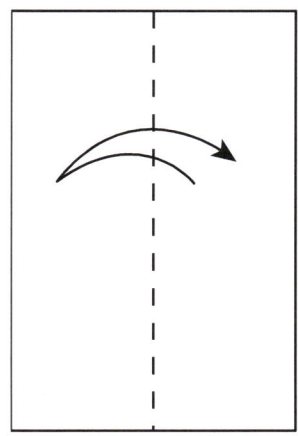

1 start with 2:3 rectangle, see page 8 for cutting instructions

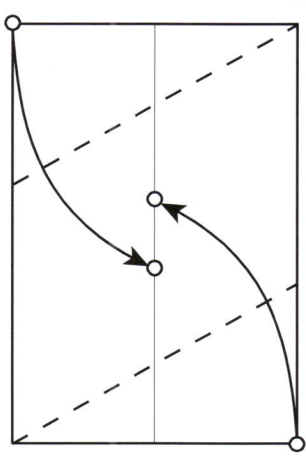

2 align marked corners to the line

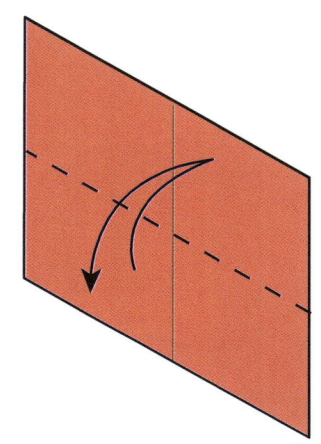

3

59

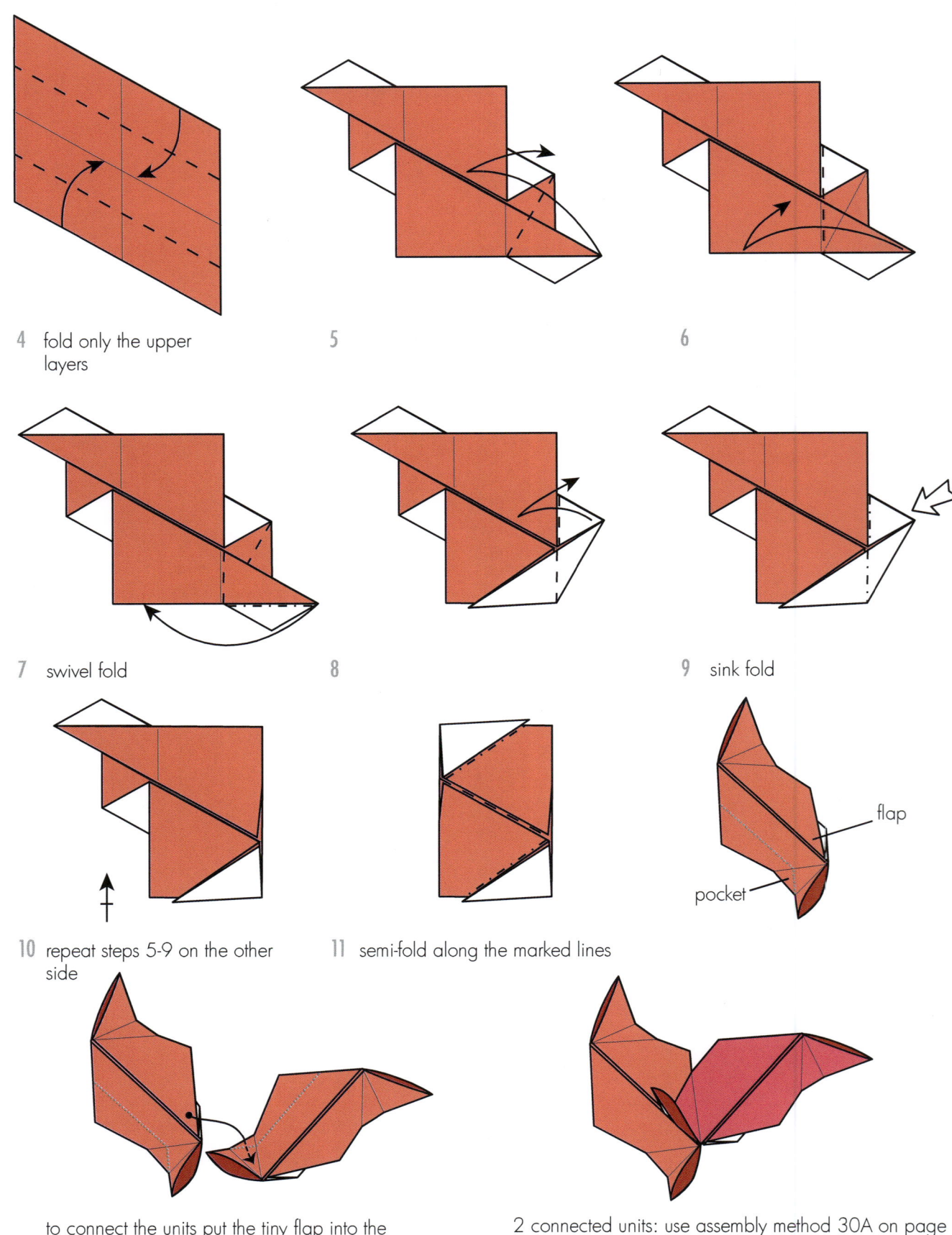

★★★
30A, 12A

6x9 cm rectangle (proportion 2:3)

CELESTINA
CURLY VARIATION

There are a lot of variations you can get from Celestina unit. Just a slight change in the unit's folding sequence can result different ornament on the complete ball's surface.

30A

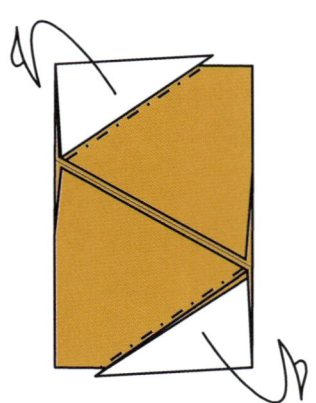

11 start with step 11 of Celestina model on page 59

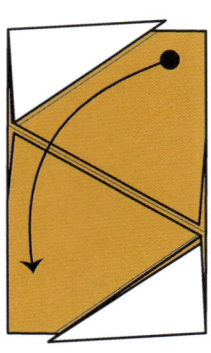

12 pull the paper as far as possible

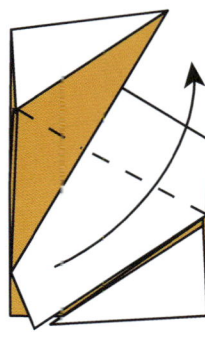

13 repeat steps 12-13 on the other side

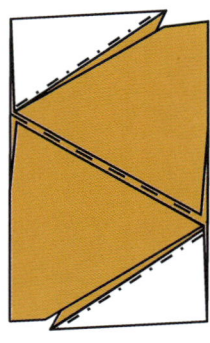

14 semi-fold along the marked lines

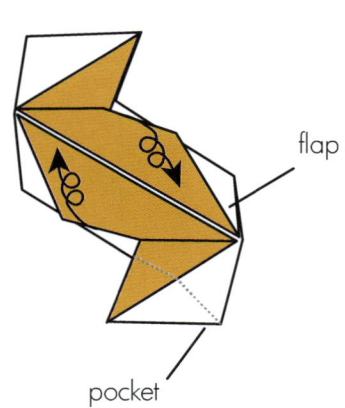

complete unit
you may additionally curl the lose flaps for floral look

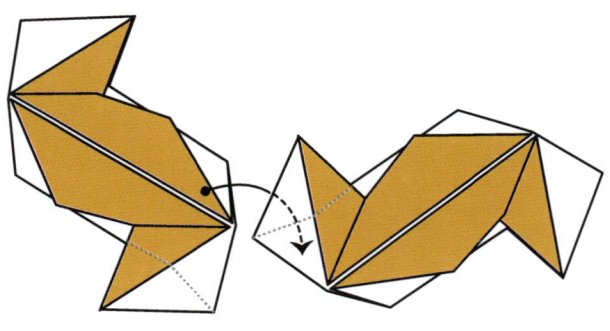

to connect the units put the tiny flap into the pocket under the petal

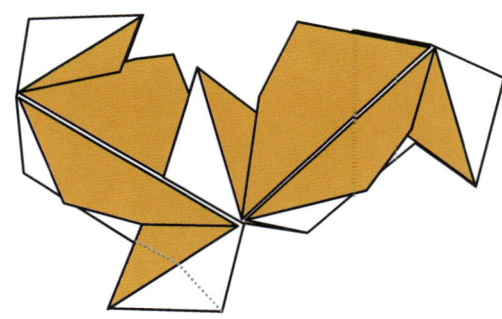

2 connected units: use assembly method 30A on page 14 or assembly method 12A on page 12

30A, 12A

6x9 cm rectangle (proportion 2:3)

CELESTINA
STAR VARIATION

One more variation of the same unit. Start with Celestina Curly unit at step 13. The units are connected the same way as the other Celestina units, using assembly method 30A on page 14 or assembly method 12A on page 12

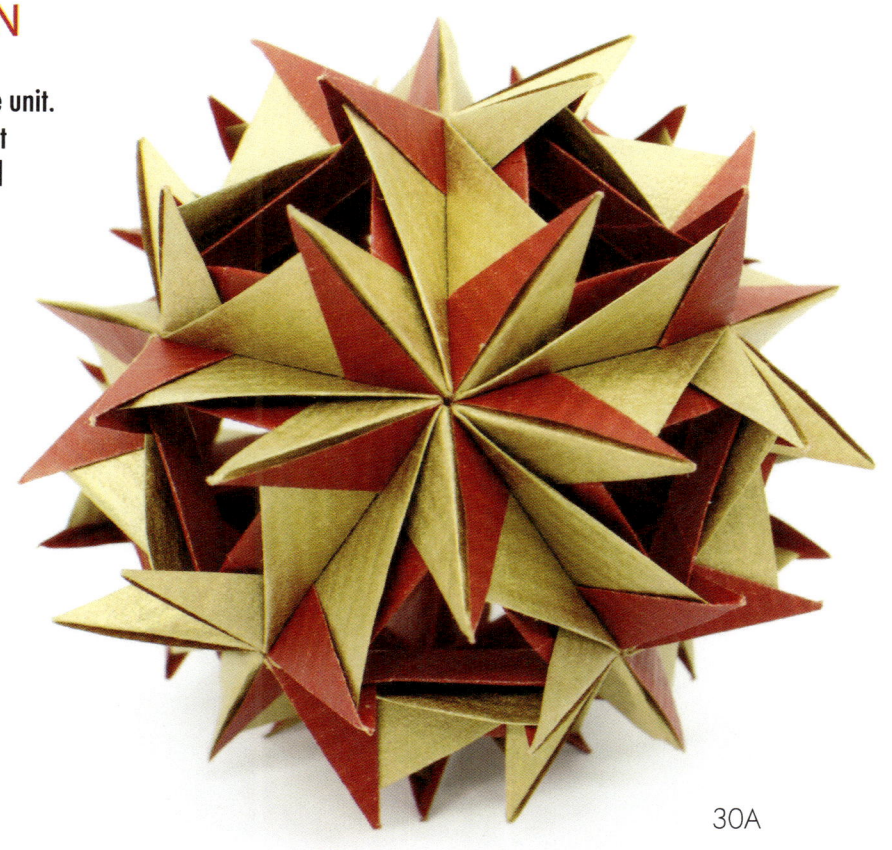

30A

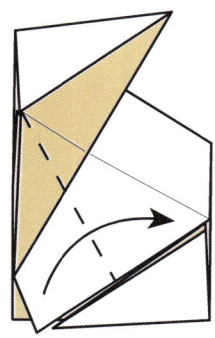

13 start with step 13 on previous page

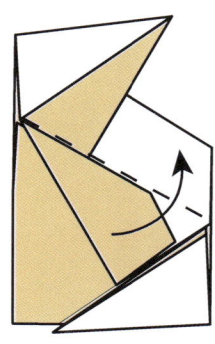

14

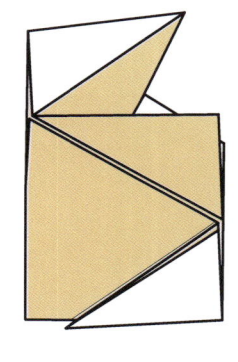

15 repeat steps 12-14 on the other side

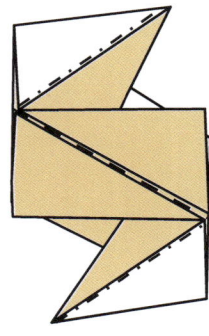

15 semi-fold the marked lines, connect the units the same way as all Celestina units

63

ICE

7x7 cm square

★★★ 30A, 12A

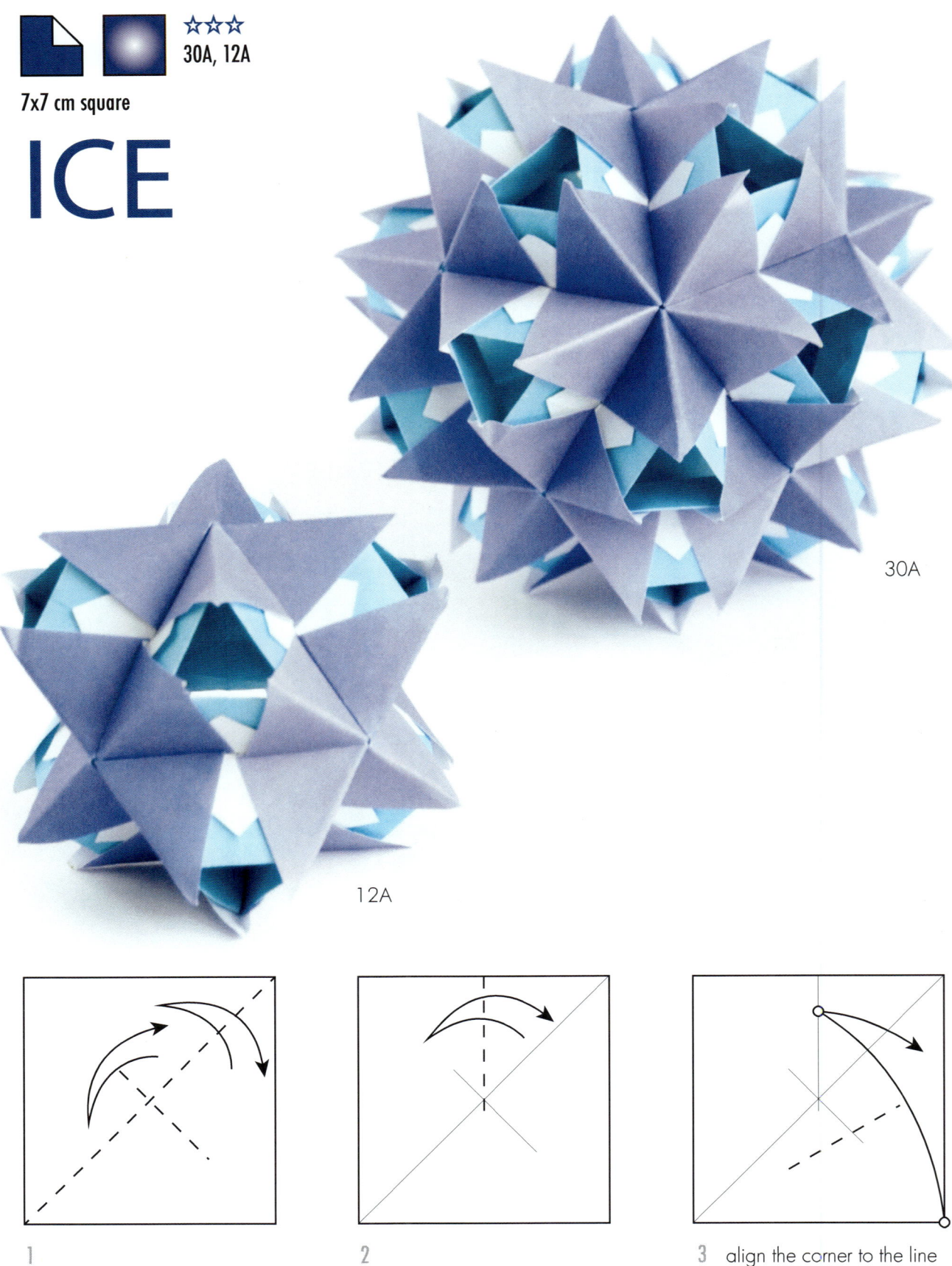

30A

12A

1

2

3 align the corner to the line and unfold

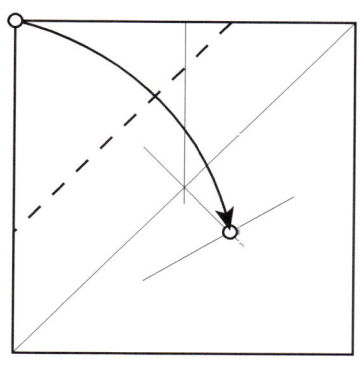
4 align the corner to the point

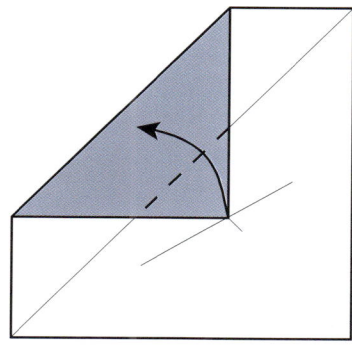
5 fold to align the underlying line

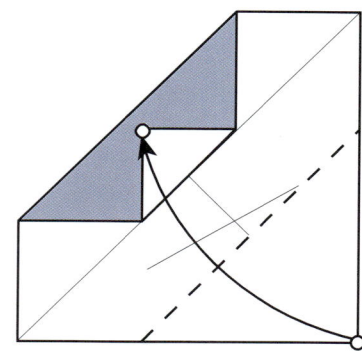
6 align the corner to the point

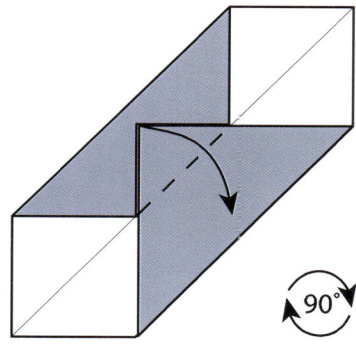
7 fold to align the underlying line

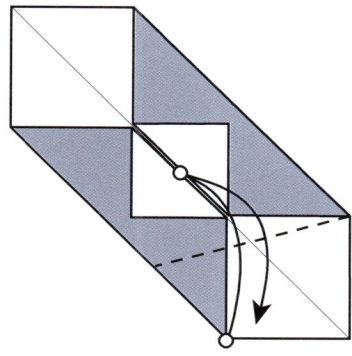
8 align the corner to the line and unfold

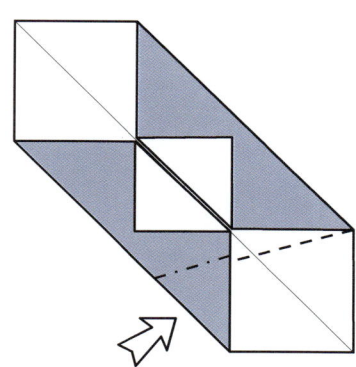
9 inside reverse fold

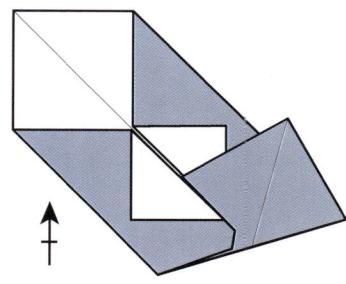
10 repeat steps 8-9 on the other side

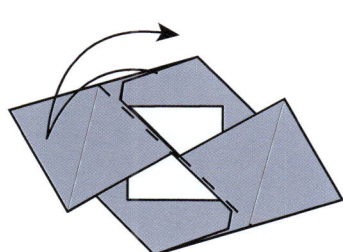
11

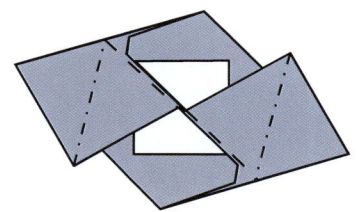
12 semi-fold the marked lines

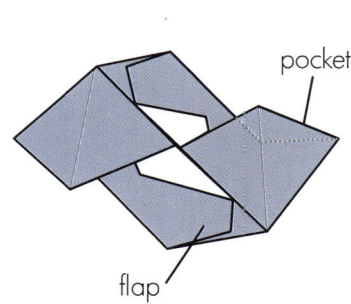
the complete unit

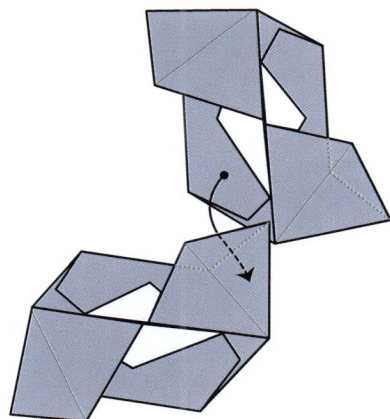
to connect 2 units insert the flap into the pocket

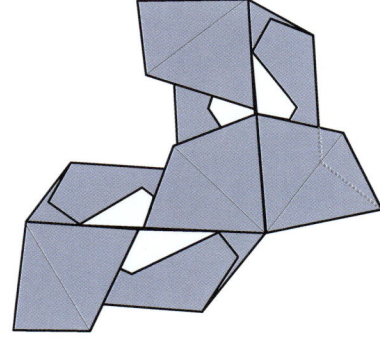
assembly methods 12A on page 12 and 30A on page 14 are the most recommended for this model, though you can also use methods 12B on page 13 and 30B on page 15

65

 ★★★
30A, 12A

7x7 cm square

ICE CREAM

30A

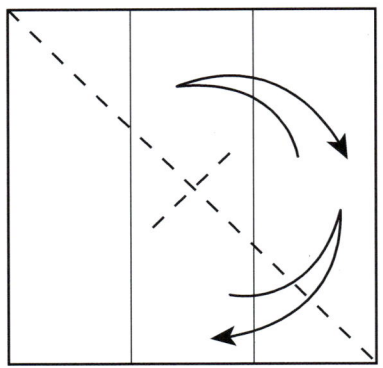

1   divide square to thirds (see cutting 2:3 rectangle on page 8 for dividing instructions)

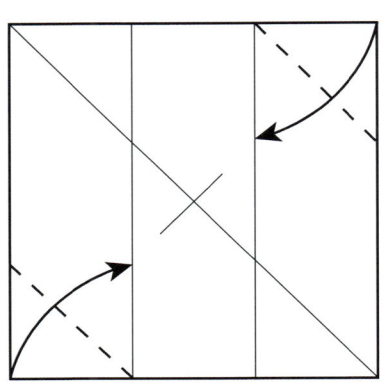

2

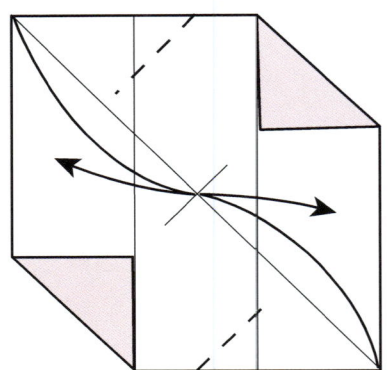

3   make pinch marks, folding corners to the center

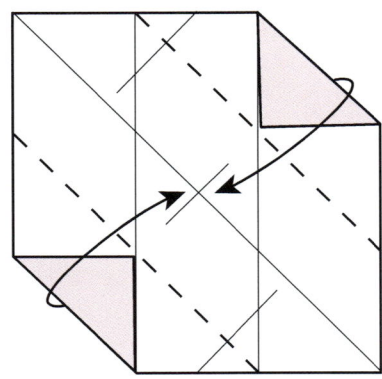

4

5

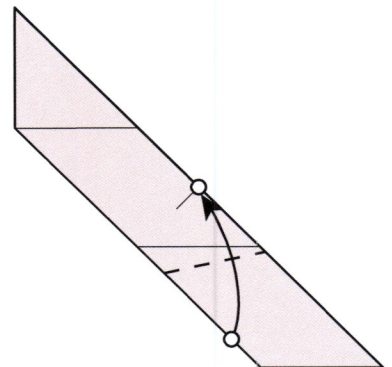

6   align point on the back with the pinch mark

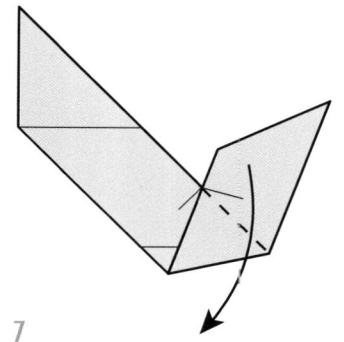

7

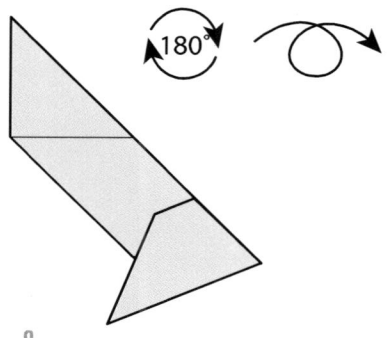

8

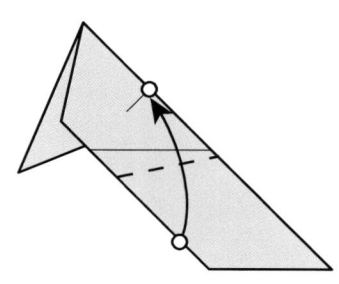

9 align point on the back with the pinch mark

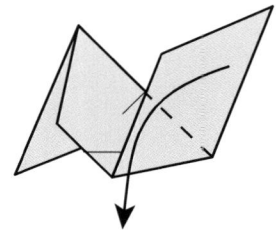

10

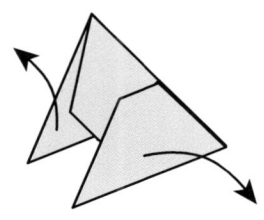

11 unfold to step 5

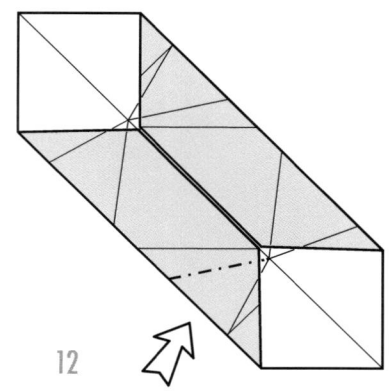

12 inside reverse fold only the marked side, the resulting figure won't be flat

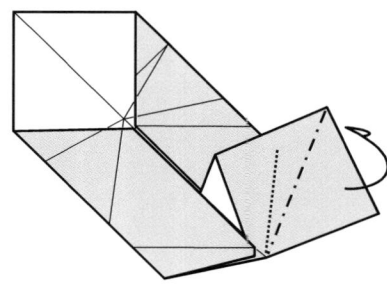

13 fold back using existing lines, figure will lie flat again

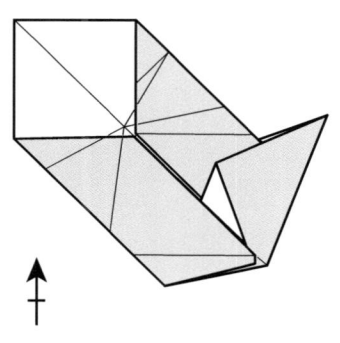

14 repeat steps 12-13 on the other side

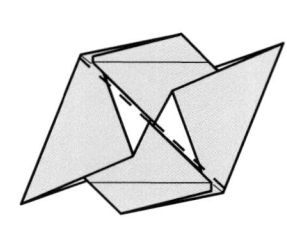

15 semi-fold along the marked lines

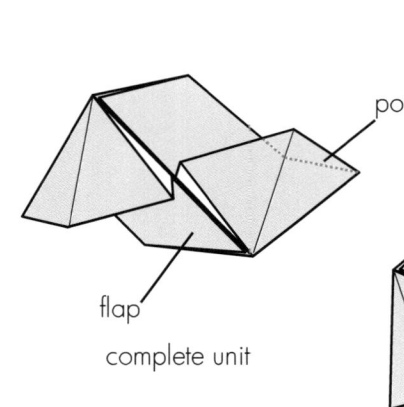

pocket

flap

complete unit

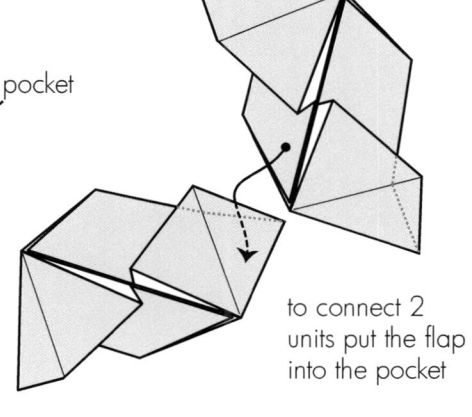

to connect 2 units put the flap into the pocket

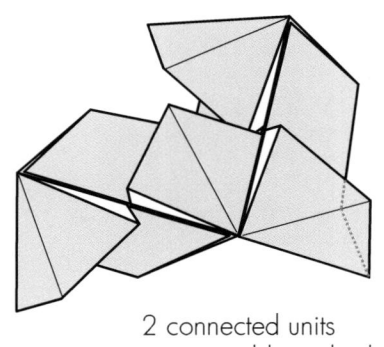

2 connected units use assembly method 30A on page 14

67

30A

7x7 cm square

CREAM

This kusudama is based on Ice Cream model but features elegant curls. Use pincers for curling the petals after you assemble the units.

30A

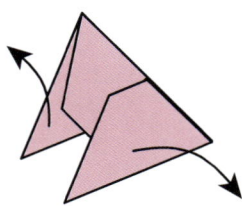

1 make Ice Cream unit untill the 11th step, unfold it to step 4 and turn over

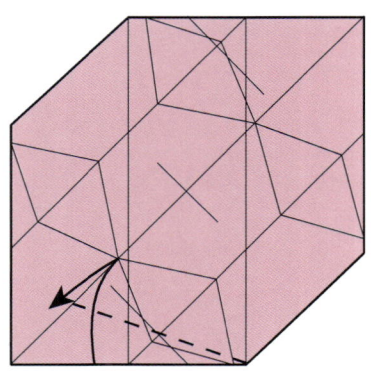

2 fold to align the border with the marked point

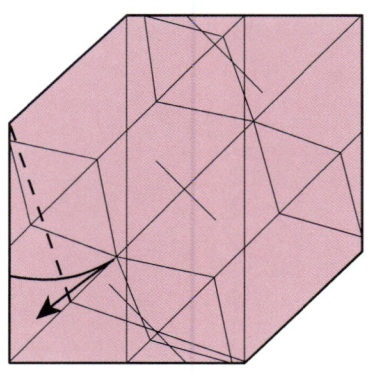

3 fold to align the border with the marked point

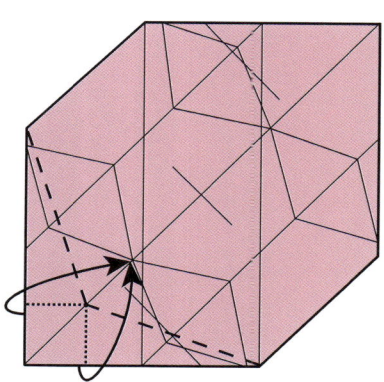

4 rabbit ear fold: try not to make the dotted creases too crisp

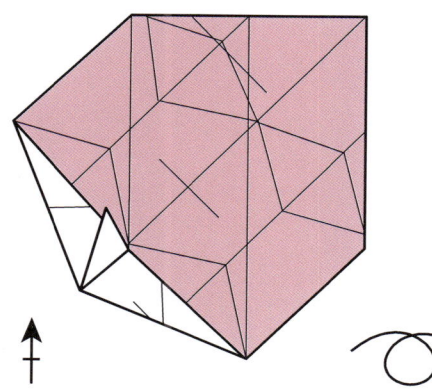

5 repeat steps 2-4 on the other side

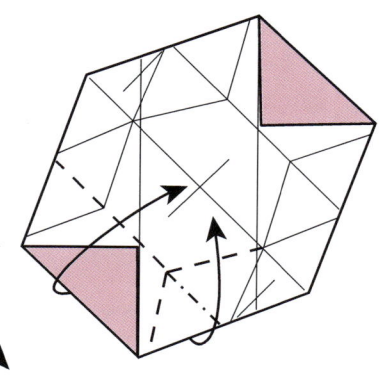

6 fold the marked lines only the figure won't be flat

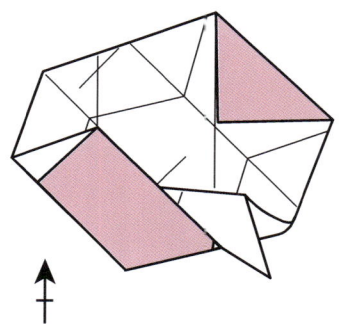

7 repeat step 6 on the other side

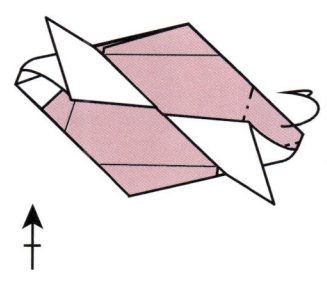

8 fold back the marked part, the side will be flat again, repeat on the other side

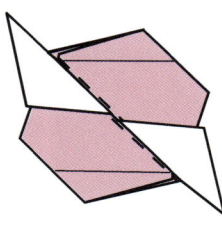

9 semi-fold the marked line

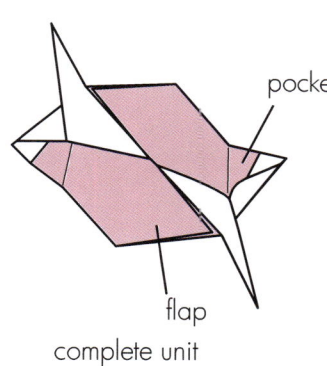

pocket

flap

complete unit

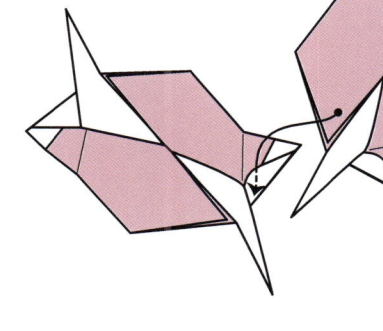

to connect 2 units
put the flap into the pocket

curl the decorative flaps a bit during the assembly so that they won't interfere with each other

2 connected units
use assembly method 30A on page 14
or assembly method 12A on page 12

7x7 cm square

★★★★
30A, 12A

SNOW QUEEN

This kusudama reminds me of the Snow Queen's castle. If you make it with contrasting paper, sharp stars will appear on the surface.

30A

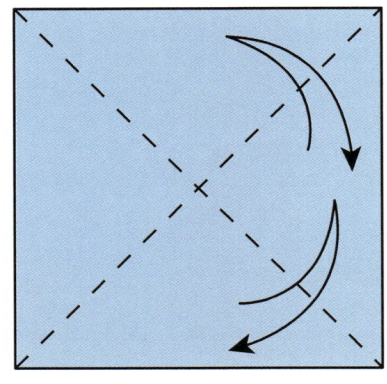

1

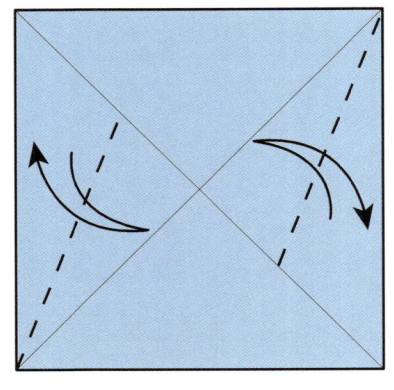

2

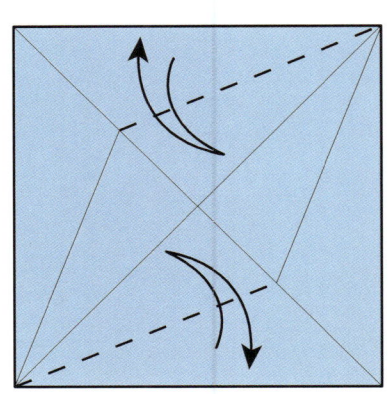

3

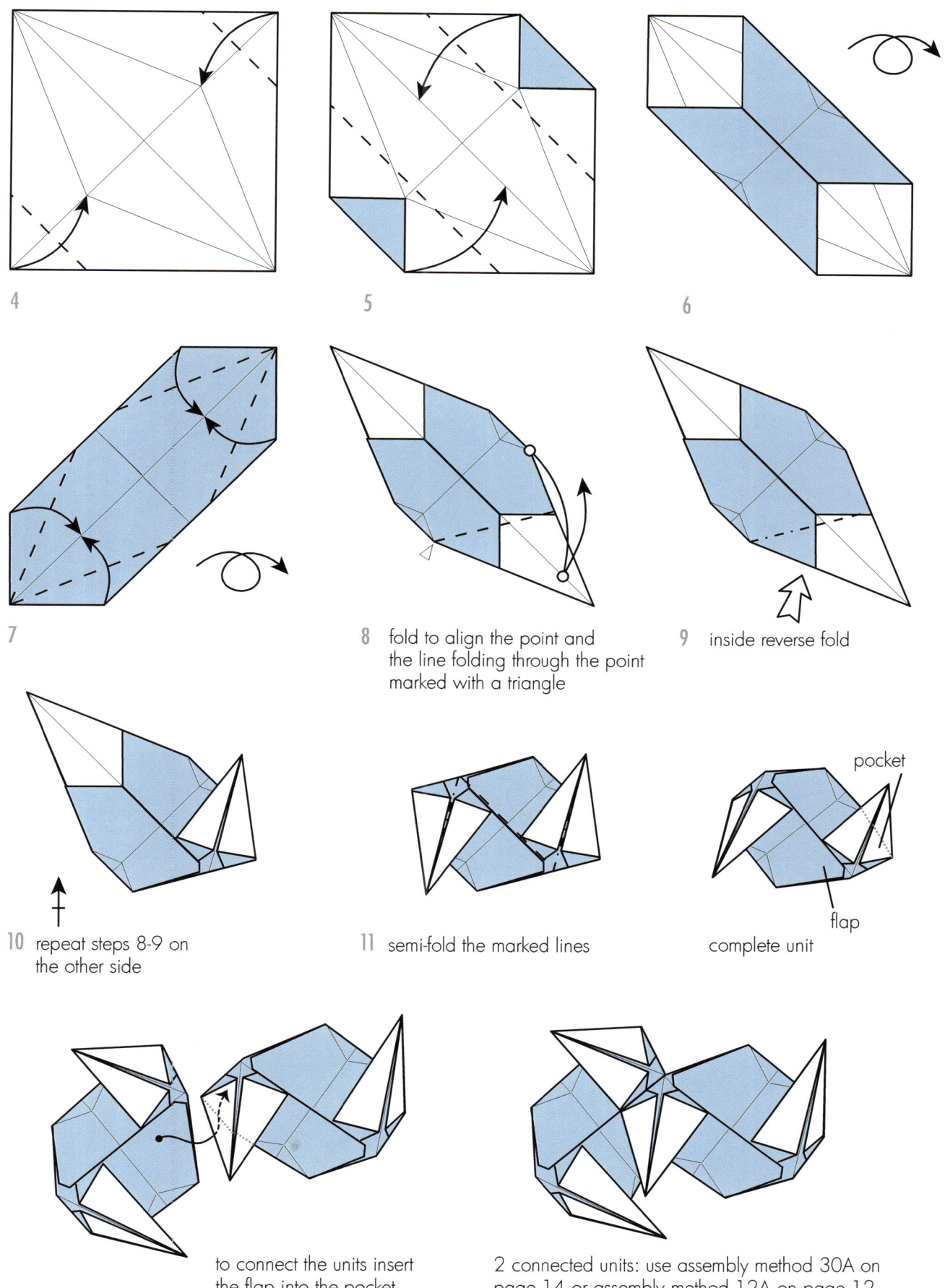

4

5

6

7

8 fold to align the point and the line folding through the point marked with a triangle

9 inside reverse fold

10 repeat steps 8-9 on the other side

11 semi-fold the marked lines

complete unit

pocket

flap

to connect the units insert the flap into the pocket

2 connected units: use assembly method 30A on page 14 or assembly method 12A on page 12

☆☆☆☆☆ 30A, 12A

10x10 cm square

JACIARA

From the Tupi Guarani language, spoken by indigenous people of southern Brazil, Jaciara means "child of the moon".

30A

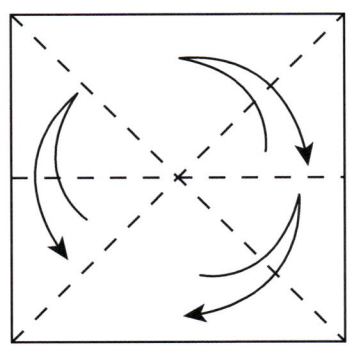

1

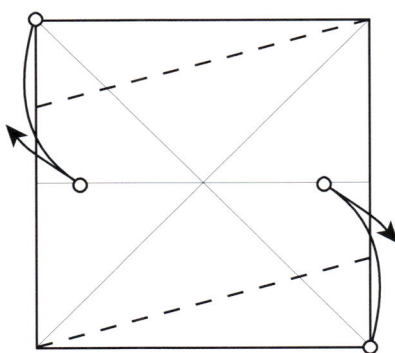

2 align corners to the lines

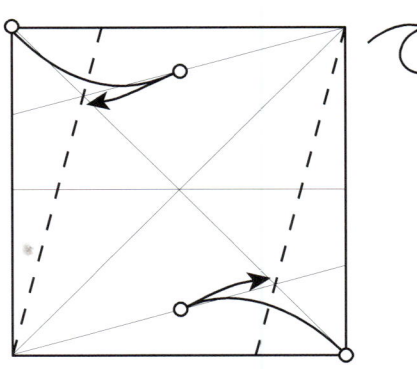

3 align corners to the lines

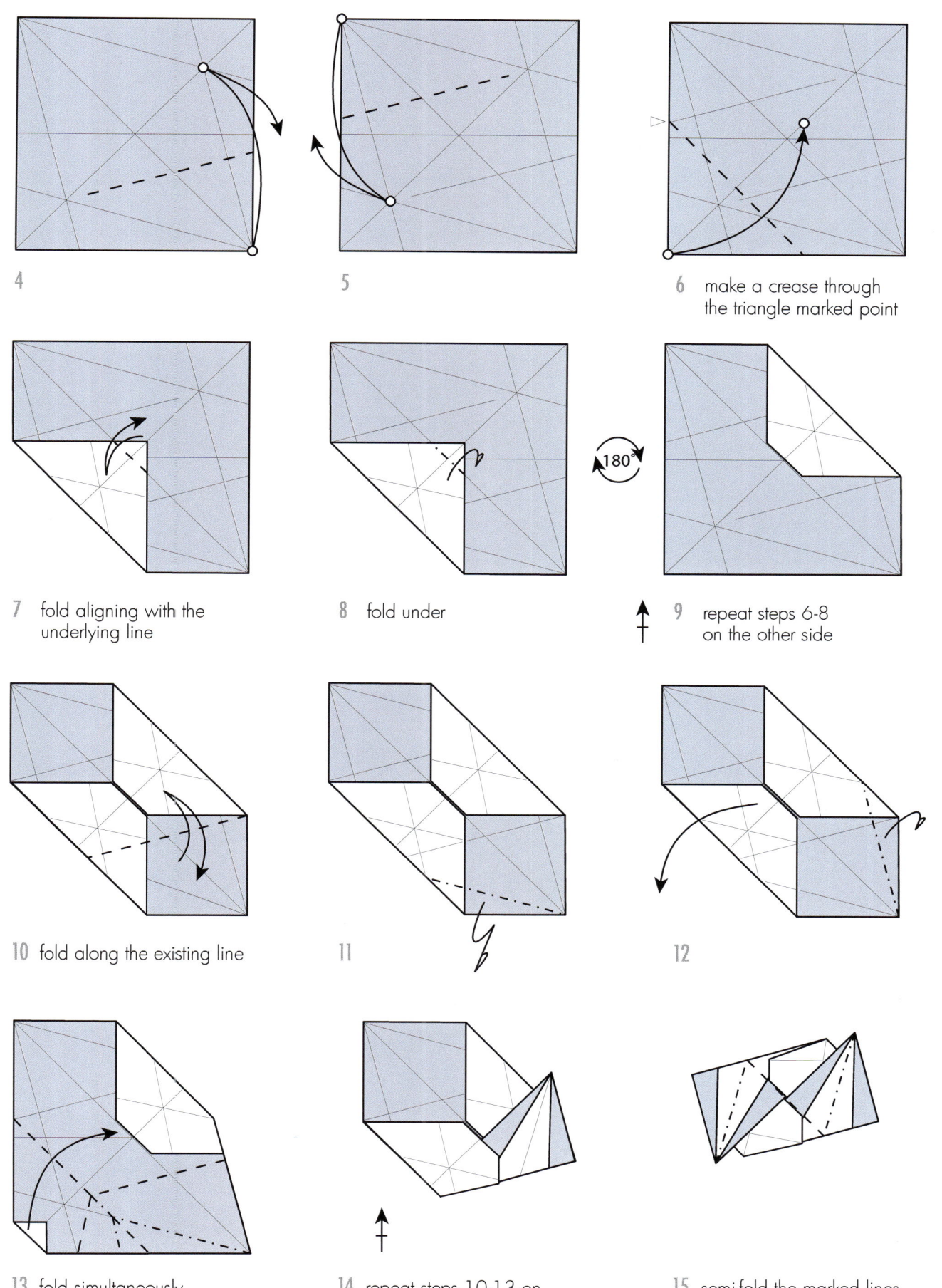

4

5

6 make a crease through the triangle marked point

7 fold aligning with the underlying line

8 fold under

9 repeat steps 6-8 on the other side

10 fold along the existing line

11

12

13 fold simultaneously

14 repeat steps 10-13 on the other side

15 semi-fold the marked lines

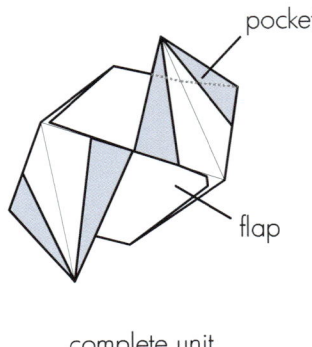

complete unit

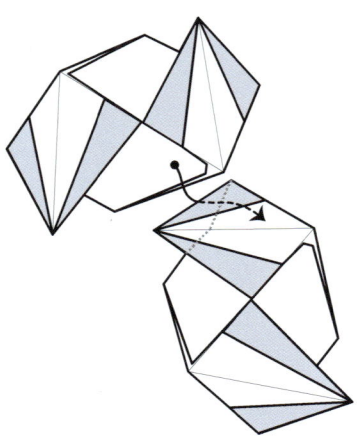

to connect the units insert the flap into the pocket

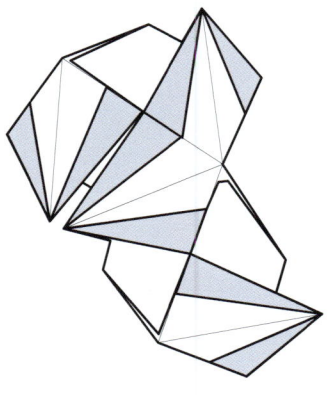

2 connected units: for assembly
use method 30A on page 14
or method 12A on page 12
or method 12B on page 13
or method 30B on page 15
the result of 30B method
is shown below

30B

VARIATION 1

The next diagrams show how to change the color distribution on the surface of the Jaciara unit

30A

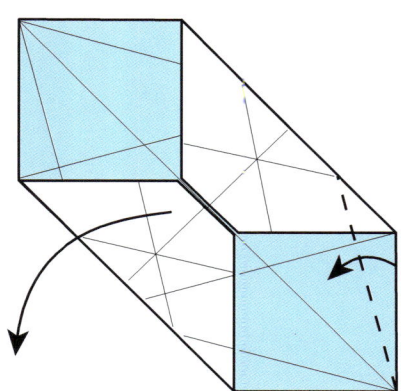

12 do this step instead of step 12 of Jaciara model then proceed with all remaining steps of the Jaciara model

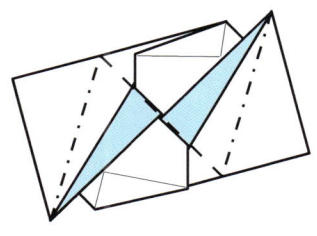

15 semi-fold the marked lines

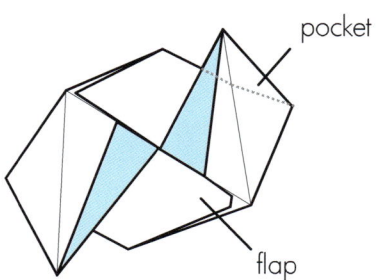

complete unit
connect the same way as Jaciara units on previous page

75

VARIATION 2

This variation seems pointless until you open the petals

30A

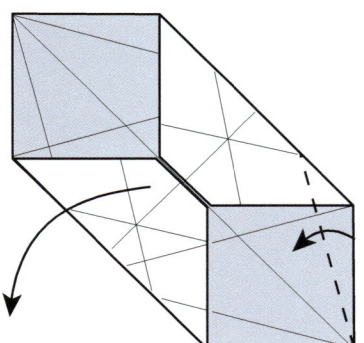

12 start with step 12 of Jaciara model

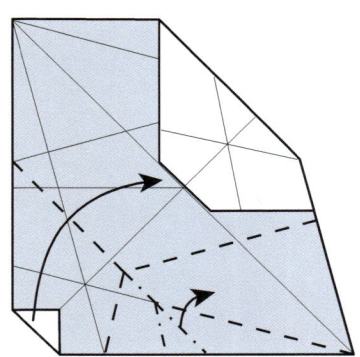

13 fold simultaneously: this fold may require practice on a larger piece of paper

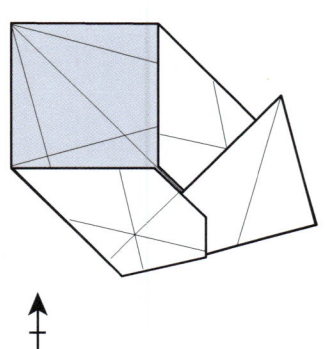

14 repeat steps 10-13 on the other side

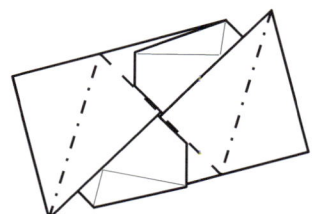

14 semi-fold the marked lines

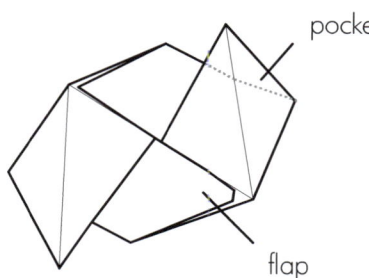

pocket

flap

complete unit

30A

curl the petals using pincers
you can curl one 'flower' or
curl all the petals

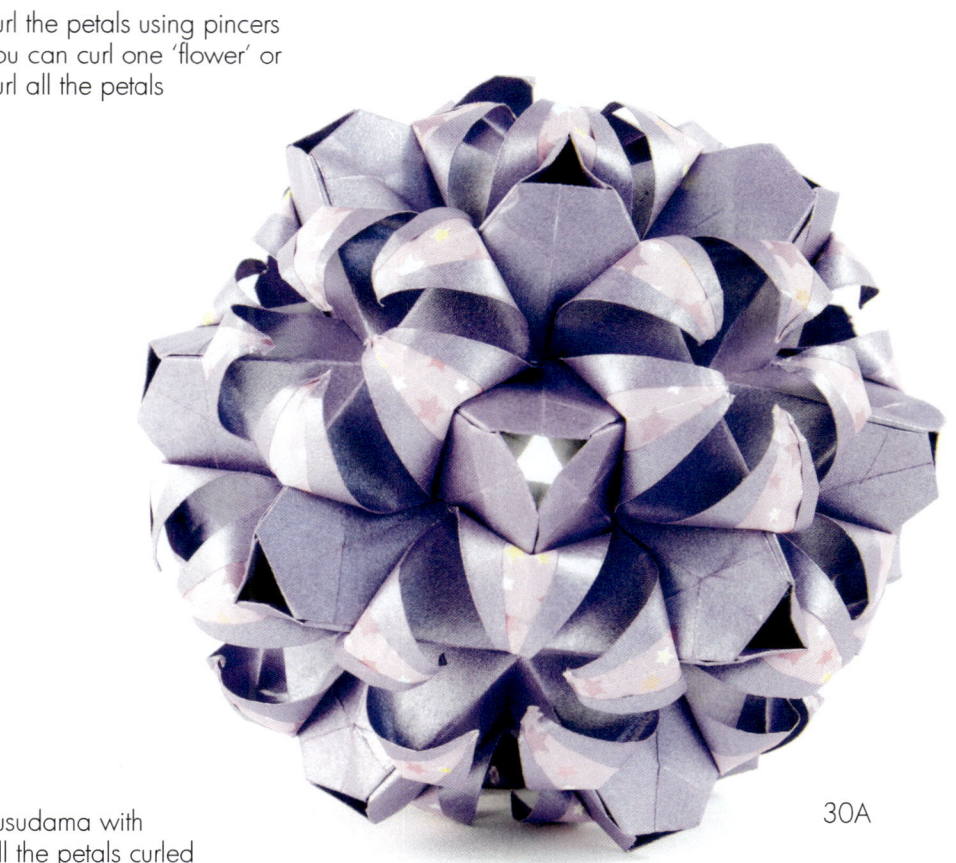

kusudama with
all the petals curled

30A

 ★★★★
30A, 12A

10x10 cm square

JACIARA
VARIABLE

This model is the sister model for Jaciara model and is indeed easier to perform. Moreover it has plenty of variations. The diagram for this model has two major parts. The first part is the base for the unit, which you can replace with another base. The diagram for the other base will be given later. The second part is for the unit itself and may be used with various bases.

30A

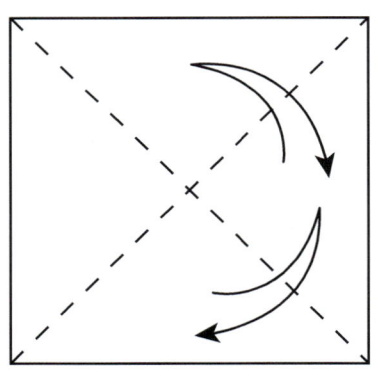

1

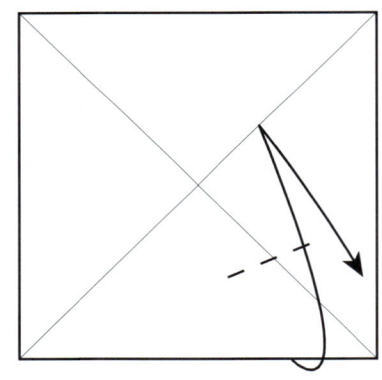

2 pinch

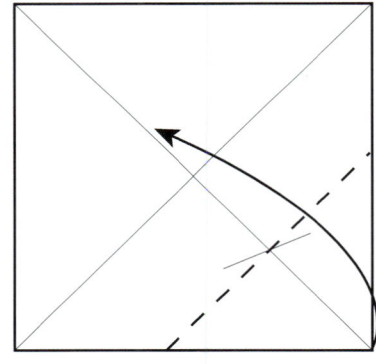

3 make the crease through the pinch aligning corner to the line

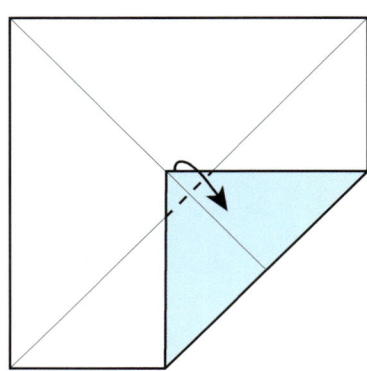

4 align to the underlying line

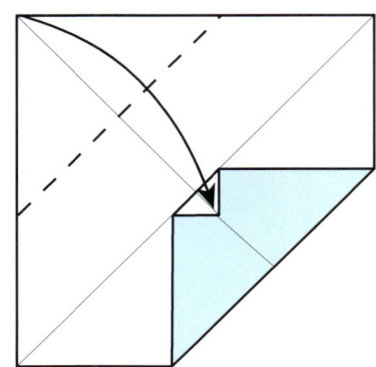

5

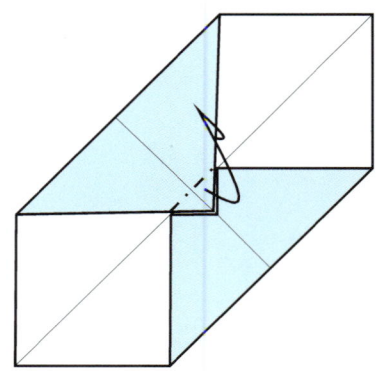

6 fold the tiny triangle inside

78

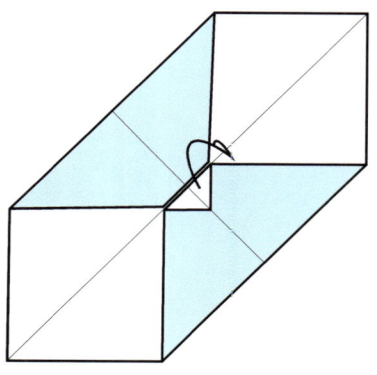

7 fold the tiny triangle inside

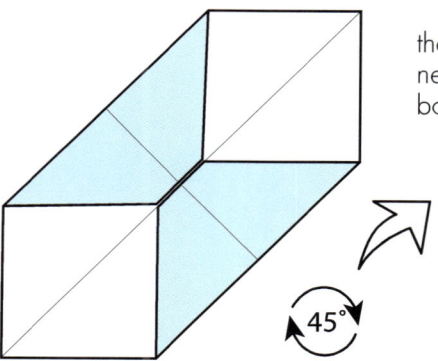

complete base

the base is complete, proceed the next steps of the diagram with the both sides of this base

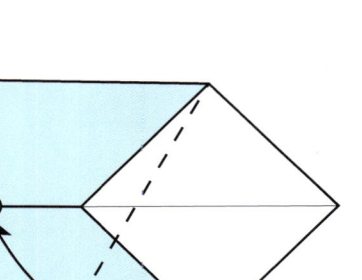

8 align point to the line

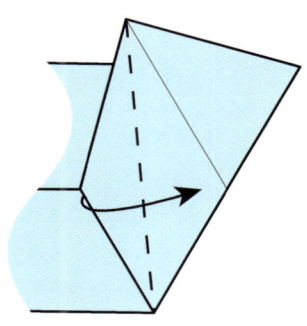

9

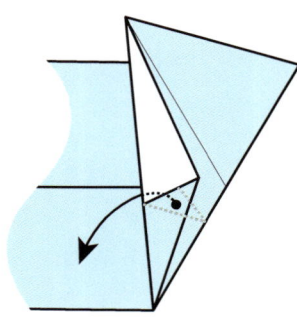

10 pull the paper from inside

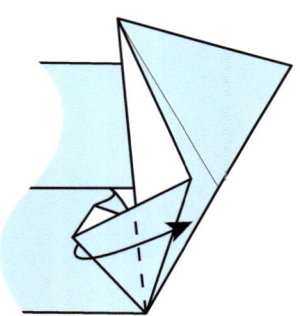

11 fold using existing crease

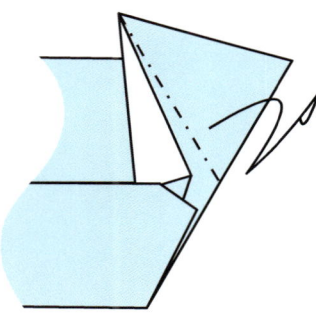

12 fold back along the existing crease and unfold

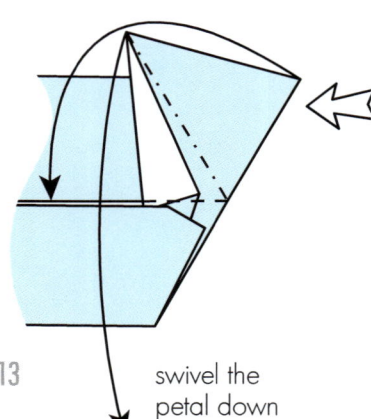

13 swivel the petal down

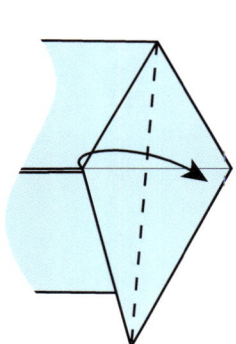

14

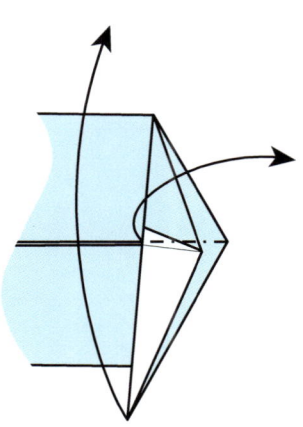

15 return the petal up opening its side

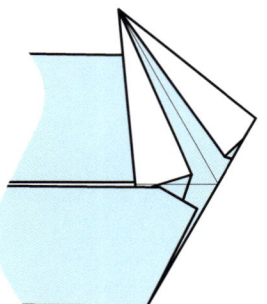

complete side: repeat 8-15 with the other side of the unit connect the same way as Jaciara

 ★★★★ 30A, 12A

10x10 cm square

JACIARA
VARIABLE

30A

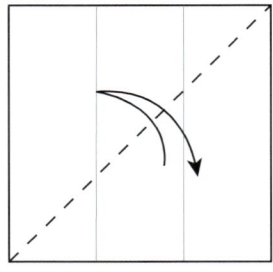

1 divide square to thirds (see cutting 2:3 rectangle on page 8 for dividing instructions)

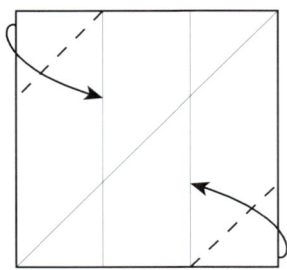

2

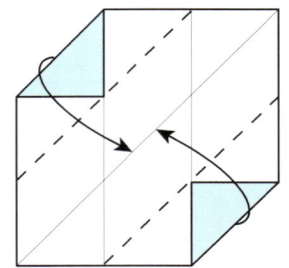

3

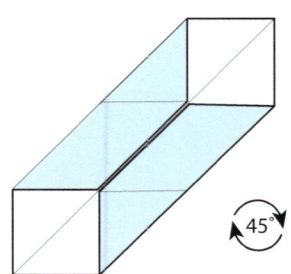

the base is complete: do steps 8-15 on the previous page to complete the unit

Printed in Great Britain
by Amazon